MW00647248

The Myth of Race
The Reality of Racism
Critical Essays

Mahmoud El-Kati

Papyrus Publishing Inc.

The Myth of Race The Reality of Racism: Critical Essays
by El-Kati, Mahmoud

ISBN: 978-0-9882883-3-1

Originally published by the Stairstep Foundation in 1993

Papyrus Publishing Inc.
Brooklyn Park, Minnesota, United States of America
PapyrusPublishing@msn.com

Cover Design by Rekhet Si-Asar

Dedication

To Yusef Mgeni – The Quiet Warrior

A good man, a kindred spirit, one with whom I have been privileged to share brotherhood in this noble struggle of our people for social justice, moral clarity, and human dignity.

To Josie R. Johnson - One of the greatest human beings I know

Yet with a steady beat, have not our weary feet... echoes the life and spirit of Josie R. Johnson. She like Frederick Douglass has engaged in "earnest struggle." Labor, sacrifice and love defines her character. I envy her diplomatic skills in dealing with this question of "race". She is a stateswoman who knows how to work both sides of the isle. Above all else, she has been the dearest of friends, whom I have known for most of my conscious life. For this I am internally blessed.

Acknowledgements

As for me, there is simply no way to express satisfactorily my sincere thanks and appreciation to the two people who have made this moment possible. The second publication of this little treatise is due primarily to two thoughtful, committed individuals. First there is Alfred Babington-Johnson founder and CEO of Stairstep Foundation Inc., a community-based organization, which has rendered a powerful service to the social health and spiritual wealth of the Twin Cities community. It was he who suggested that I refine a somewhat extemporaneous speech that he heard me make at a conference on "race". This was a conference called by then Mayor of Minneapolis, Sharon Sayles-Belton some 20 years ago. This gathering was well attended by a good cross-section of informed voices from the Twin Cities: Civil rights workers, educators, business leaders, city and county workers, and a smattering of youth. For me, it was one of my typical on the edge, evocative talking points message, minus good form. Babington-Johnson was struck by something in the content of my remarks. Accordingly, he suggested that I let him look at a copy of "my speech" of which there were no such thing, but wildly scattered notes on three sheets of paper. He suggested that I write something more formal and give it to him. Within the blink of an eye, that speech was turned into *The Myth of Race The Reality of Racism*, the first publication of the Stairstep Board of Directors. This publication was used in part to help carryout their mission, which is to enhance the general education of its community on this pregnant question. Also my endless thanks goes to Babington-Johnson's administrative assistant at the time, Menia Buckner, a multi-talented super industrious dynamo who typed every page of the original script.

The second individual I feel compelled to hail and salute is Janet Williams, a friend and long time neighbor. The fact we have a second edition of *The Myth of Race The Reality of Racism* is due to her singular and passionate commitment to creative education and social justice. Janet Williams is the driving force at the other end of this projectile, which was launched 20 years ago. Her diligent, personal, almost religious zeal in making things happen is amazing. Janet brought her enormous array of talents and network of connections to the fore. Except for the printing of the book itself, she has been the major organizer and director of this project. She along with our dependable and multitask oriented publisher, Anura Si-Asar, Papyrus Publishing Inc., are two sides of the same horse. They took a page out of the book of Nelson Mandela; "It is always impossible - until it's done."

Finally, I think that there is one other necessary thing to say about the matter. There has been a 20-year stretch since the original publication. Earlier last year, Papyrus Publishing had been exploring the idea of printing a book on "race" and racism in light of a new currency regarding this question, though with no concrete plan or timeline for its release. And then one fine Tuesday, Janet Williams surprisingly approached me, informing me that 2003 was the anniversary of *The Myth of Race The Reality of Racism* and that something should be done to acknowledge the occasion. She explained how and why it meant so much to her personally and some of her associates. I agreed to cooperate, though at the time, nothing could have been farther from my mind. We thought it would be appropriate to begin the process by contacting Alfred Babington-Johnson of Stairstep, the first publisher and of course Papyrus shall we say, "the rest is history".

In addition, a heart felt thanks to the St. Paul Foundation - Facing Race Initiative for their generous support in funding this project.

Contents

Appendix

Foreword

Some people and some moments grace your life in such a way as to make an indelible impact. Mahmoud El-Kati is such a one, and a speech he gave twenty years ago was such a moment. If you have met him you will agree – he moves through life and the community as an understated, but powerful presence.

I first met Mahmoud El-Kati in the summer of 1968. I had just completed my senior year at Howard University, and I came to Minneapolis to work with my brother Tafi in an intriguing effort called the Institute of African American Studies. The Institute taught seven-week courses reviewing the narrative of Black people being brought to these shores and recounting the steps of the passage from then to contemporary life.

There were a handful of teachers that shouldered the responsibility of teaching the classes in settings that ranged from corporate board chambers to suburban living rooms. The premier lecturer was definitely Mahmoud. He wasn't loud and not overly animated, but there was richness in his presentation and a breadth in his knowledge that was fascinating. It seemed he could go on for hours reciting, word for word, the insights offered by W.E.B. DuBois, or the challenging pronouncements of Frederick Douglass, or the gritty but eloquent renderings of James Baldwin. Mahmoud was the man!

Small wonder that as the calendar moved ahead by months, then years, then decades, Mahmoud continued to be in great demand. All over the country folk warmed to his messages and sub points regarding the wonderful cultural contribution of Black America; the importance of building institutions; and the critical requirement of including youth in discussions and in community actions.

So I was one of many fans who gathered whenever the good professor was known to be holding forth. On one such occasion, over twenty years ago, I was riveted by a presentation he gave on racism. I must tell you I had grown weary by the 1990s of what seemed to be a continuous and pointless fixation on discussing racism. This was quite different.

The unique aspect of the discussion by Mahmoud was that he defined racism in a way that created a platform for serious people to discuss and take action. He said, "Racism is prejudice plus power." Eureka! This would allow real dialog and could lead to real change. If someone was really interested in doing something about racism, they had to commit to changing the power relationships.

I raced up to join the growing crowd of autograph seekers following the presentation. "Can I have a copy of your speech manuscript?" I asked. He demurred saying that he just spoke from a general set of notes. I pressed him on the importance of the wisdom he had shared and suggested that he create a written version.

When he acquiesced, the fruit of his labors compelled me to ask permission to pursue publication. The result was of such value we now gratefully embrace the reprint. The value has not been diminished.

Reverend Alfred Babington-Johnson
President/CEO Stairstep Foundation

Introduction

Two decades ago in 1993, as he has reconstructed it from the archives of his own memory, Professor Mahmoud El-Kati delivered a singularly memorable speech at the Minneapolis Convention Center. He did so in response to an invitation from the Minneapolis Initiative Against Racism (MIAR), a group of community leaders and activists co-founded by City Council member Sharon Sayles Belton, whose historic mayoral campaign that year would make her the first woman and first African American mayor in the city's history. The group's initiative against racism was pragmatic as well as multi-pronged: it proposed to change the dynamics of public policy and public debate about race and racism, and Mahmoud El-Kati's long-lived and multidimensional political and intellectual leadership made him an inevitable choice to guide such change. Against the backdrop of the first year of Bill Clinton's presidency and of local newspaper headlines fixated both on a Minneapolis murder rate at an all time high and on grim evidence that the country's national crack cocaine epidemic was raging here also, the speech El-Kati delivered from a loose sheaf of notes concerned itself very little with such pressuring immediacies.

Instead, *The Myth of Race, the Reality of Racism*, like so much of his incessant teaching over the past half century, attacked with controlled ferocity the dichotomies of consciousness from which so many of the contradictions of our lived experience derive. Using the tools of a philosopher-dialectician on the one hand, and those of an empirical psychologist on the other, El-Kati's anatomy of our nation's racial pathology aligned itself operationally with a famous psychoanalyst's prior recognition that "no one can flatter himself that he is immune to the spirit of his own epoch, or even that he possesses a full understanding of it. Irrespective of our conscious convictions, each one of us, without exception, being a particle of the general mass, is somewhere attached to, colored by, or even

1

undermined by the spirit which goes through the mass. Freedom stretches only as far as the limits of our consciousness."

Always attuned to the expressive powers of language and the poetry of the apt quotation, El-Kati grounded his address in the contemporary prophetic insights of James Baldwin and, looking backwards, in the nineteenth century visions of Frederick Douglass and Frenchman Alexis De Tocqueville. From twentieth century anthropologist Ashley Montagu (*Man's Most Dangerous Myth: The Fallacy of Race*) and cultural historian Jacques Barzun (*Race: A Study in Modern Superstition*), he distilled for his audience the centuries-old history of race-thinking and race-ruling as conjoined ideas and institutions that reflect, above all, the realities of power, the relationships between dominant and subordinate groups in history.

From today's perspective in a media-soaked world all too familiar with the genomic footprints of human DNA and the tracings of the double-helix back to an African origin, it has become considerably easier to accept the notion that, like nations, "races" are what Benedict Anderson calls "imagined communities"—social constructs, fabrications made in history by historical forces, and which acquire meaning and reality only in relation to identifiable Others. But it is also easy to forget that just twenty years ago, when El-Kati spoke, the explanatory power of race had not yet been deconstructed thoroughly enough to prevent the bestselling publication the following year of Richard Herrnstein and Charles Murray's, *The Bell Curve: Intelligence and Class Structure in American Life*, wherein the ancient logics of racial inferiority and domination were reconfigured in full display, with all the illusory trappings of authoritative social science.

Today it remains impossible to deny that the science of human genetics—to which we look anxiously for breakthroughs in the fights against cancer and Alzheimers' disease and crime--is still developmentally young; and as a troublesome corollary of the unwinding Age of Obama, the long debates over race are not yet over. Mahmoud El-Kati's staunchest service to his original audience was to teach them the lesson of eternal vigilance in intellectual as well as institutional struggles for freedom. As an American historian of an even earlier generation once told his audience in *The Education of Henry Adams*, "a teacher affects eternity; he can never tell where his influence stops." In El-Kati's case, the original influence of that 1993 speech galvanized the Rev. Alfred Babington Johnson to instigate the translation of the teacher's loose sheaf of notes into a finely wrought "critical essay" that the Stairstep Foundation and Challenge Productions first brought into print. With the passage of time, widening circles of influence galvanized Janet Williams to create, together with Papyrus Publishing, this occasion two decades later for introducing El-Kati's ideas to another generation at yet another juncture in eternity. For all these reasons, the appearance once more in print of his inspirational words ought to be regarded not merely as a reprint, but as a renewal.

Professor John S. Wright
Morse-Amoco Distinguished Teaching Professor of African American Studies and English, University of Minnesota

The Myth of "Race" and The Reality of Racism: A Thesis

The African, or more precisely, the Ashanti proverb says that "if you know the beginning well, the end won't trouble you." If you know the original sin, then you know and understand why things are as they are today - whether you are an optimist or a pessimist. If you are an optimist you are not troubled at all. If you are a pessimist you can be troubled only by the challenge to face the truth. I insist that there is something fundamental about our present fortunes, which derives from what should be defined as original sin. This sin called racial slavery has produced its own consequences and is so profoundly a part of the body politic of America. It was George Will, the noted conservative pundit, the eminent political commentator and pontifical voice for everything, who said that "everything that's true is derivative and everything that's not is false". My bias against contemporary conservative thought notwithstanding, I concur with that statement. This is a good recommendation for respecting the meaning and value of history. Albert Einstein said it best, "The distinction that we make between the past, present and future is a stubborn illusion."

Fearless Candor

James Baldwin, a prophet of our own times, has admonished us to accept the fact that "nothing can be solved that can't be faced." He proclaimed, "Black and white Americans, for excellent reasons of their own, haven't the faintest desire to look back, because they view the past as quite horrible, and it will remain horrible, so long as they refuse to assess it honestly." We half consciously deny our past, he said. He went on to say, in so many words, that it is so heinous, this past, "so unspeakable and in such bad taste that it defies all categories and all definitions". Baldwin's common sense observation that "the most dangerous creation in any society is that man who has nothing to lose" is a caveat that is well worth heeding.

However, long before James Baldwin there was Frederick Douglass, the human rights champion as well as the most democratic of 19th century America who declared that, "The American people have this lesson to learn. That where justice is denied, where poverty is enforced, and ignorance prevails, where any one class of people are made to feel that society is an organized conspiracy to rob, oppress, and degrade them, neither persons nor property will be safe. Hungry men will eat, desperate men will commit crimes, and outraged men will seek revenge." In this connection with the original National sin, which is racism, which springs from the doctrine of white supremacy. This recurring theme goes back to the founding of the Republic. In the 1840s, the very insightful French writer Alexis De Tocqueville opined, "If there are ever great social revolutions in America, it will be solely because of the presence of the African people. Revolutions grow out of conditions of inequality, not equality." De Tocqueville was a great admirer of "American democracy", but could not avoid its most obvious flaw, the institution of Negro enslavement. Along that line of thinking, we have the premonition of Thomas Jefferson: "I believe that slavery is an exercise of the most boisterous passions, of unremitting despotism on the one hand, and degrading submission on the other. It teaches white children to be tyrants after the pattern of their parents. It destroys the will to work in white men, and above all, it robs man of God's greatest gift, and that is the gift of liberty. Indeed I tremble for my country when I reflect that God is just, and that His justice cannot sleep forever." Early on both De Tocqueville and Jefferson shared an instinctive foreboding, which resembles a Greek Tragedy. The Achilles Heel of the American Republic then and now is the lack of social justice for its second oldest population - African descended people. We must leave aside for a moment, the indigenous population, because they weren't a part of the Republic. They were defined outside of it, hence, "Indian Reservations". There have been two seismic shifts in the history of the still young Republic – The Civil War of the 19th century and The Civil Rights Movement of the 20th century. A part of the American character comes from the results of these critical events. Black Americans have been at the center of the struggle for De Tocqueville's true "American Democracy". Curiously they have the most sustained examples of Jefferson's "Tree of liberty...a little rebellion is its natural manure."

Given the growing awareness that we now have about the peoples in the "Global Village", it remains astonishing that so many of us otherwise enlightened people do not accept the inter relatedness of humankind, even more so of Americans, "as the last and best hope for mankind". It is an inescapable reality that the world and the people in it are interdependent. According to James Baldwin: "The world is not white. It is not black either. The future of this world depends on everyone and that future depends on, to what extent, and by what means, we liberate ourselves from a vocabulary which cannot now, bear the weight of reality." To create a new and responsible vocabulary that respects reality as it is. This is the great challenge of our time. "Let the word suit the action and the action suit the word," cried Voltaire, or was it Socrates?

Adding to the Confusion

All definitions are arbitrary. And in the final analysis the name of a thing must mean something. By racism, I mean "white supremacy." Nielly Fuller put it well, "If you don't understand the doctrine of 'white supremacy' you are going to be confused about everything else in American society." I would strongly suggest that we do not do what the popular elocutionist, the late - and in some ways great - Barbara Jordan did at the 1992 Democratic Party National Convention. Ms. Jordan at the time, a Texas-Democrat in the US House of Representatives, matter-of-factly stated, "Black racism is just as bad as white racism." It is this kind of irresponsible, displaced and timid rhetoric that contributes nothing to understanding, but contributes mightily to the confusion over the definition and reality of racism. That statement by Ms. Jordan was blatantly untrue. As Frederick Douglass would put it, "If she is sensible, she is insincere and if she is sincere, she is insensible." Barbara Jordan was a former congressperson and well-trained lawyer who has presumably studied the Constitution and the history of legal oppression as well as culturally based racism in America. She was a southerner, and a Black southerner as well, born and bred in the terrifying teeth of "white supremacy" (The cause of racism). She knew what racism was, but refused to face this unalterable fact. She earned her law degree from Texas Southern University in Houston. This is a school was established in 1943 to keep "Negroes" out of the all white University of Texas at Austin. Ms. Jordan referred to some non-existent or invisible "Black racism", without explaining what she meant, i.e.: When did it emerge? How is such "Black racism" structured in society? How does it work? Who controls the resources and power to exercise such "racism"? How are whites victimized by it? Who were these Black people who orchestrated such a system against white America? Barbara Jordan represents a significant faction of the Black middle class, same as the white middle class, not being able to afford candor on the question of "race". Her class orientation, not to mention the concocted self-deception that this mindset invents, keeps her from acknowledging that the operational words for racism are power and oppression. Racism is first and foremost, a function of power. People, such as Barbara Jordan and their unwillingness to face the facts, add much to the avoidance of the truth. There is but one system of racism in this country and that system was initiated by and remains in the hands of European-Americans. The Founding Fathers of the US assured that racism would be a part of the equation backed by the power of the State and all major institutions of the Republic. Racism means dominance, an unshared power relationship, in which the state is often involved. Nazi Germany, Australia, New Zealand, the Republic of South Africa, and before their emergence in history, the United States of America are prime examples of state sponsored racism. "Negro" Slavery is an example of this type of subordination. Under the first article in the U.S. Constitution we have one of the earliest systematic and legalistic expressions of racism in the modern world. The 3/5th clause, Article I, Sections 3 and 9 of the U.S. Constitution is an explicit block in the edifice of American-style State sponsored racism. There is no counterpart of such power among African-American people in the past or present. In America, certain people within the white population are responsible for the oppression of all African people in this country, historically and contemporarily. They are the elites (south and north) who established this system in 1787 and bequeathed it to subsequent white generational leaders. The ideology of white supremacy, which produce "the white man's burden", "manifest destiny", "city of the hill", "American exceptionalism" all of these slogans are akin to this doctrine, that is the overriding ideology of European superiority. Later, this spirit of superiority led to the rise of the Third Reich and Hilter's Nazi Germany. A kinship doctrine was implemented in the U.S. and in South Africa. White supremacy is a modern world western European construction. It is national and international in scope.

Thanks to the Barbara Jordans of this world, racism has now become a loaded term. Since the rather measured achievements of the Civil Rights Movement, and the new and false claims that we are now a non-racist or post-racial society, racism can mean anything we want it to mean without a meaningful context. The legal triumph of the Civil Rights Movement exercised some of the most blatant, shameless and reprehensible racist and contradictory aspects of American society. As a result many middle class white Americans (to keep up appearances) have repudiated the most simple-minded and outrageous manifestations of racism: "All Negroes look alike," and "They all have rhythm," and "They all are thieves" and "They all smell bad". There is no longer the publicly or legally arranged "white over Black" or "first by birth" caste lines. Coupled with National and local governments dismantling southern de jure racism, white Americans, put simply, within the blink of an eye, are now no longer racist. Within a millisecond they have cast off centuries of beliefs, customs, habits, myths, religious and legal systems and thus America is no longer a race-ridden society. Virulent, overt, mad dog racism has gone out of style. Now it is Black people's turn to be racist. The mouse, supposedly, is now chasing the cat. There is now something called "reverse racism", "reverse discrimination", and "The race card". No one quite knows how this happens. Words are curious things. You can create anything with them, even things that do not exist. The French writer was correct: "Words are like God turned loose in the flesh." Labeling everybody racist is no way to deal with this very specific and spooky phenomenon (white supremacy), which continues to threaten the bulk of the human family. We now define "race" as only a personal reality. This makes everybody racist, irrespective of history, culture, religion, or any aspect of social life. There is really no way for Black people, even if they tried to play "the race card" or even the president if he or she is Black can't play "the race card". There is no structure to support such actions. Only whites can do that.

The core reality of racism is this - it is a function of power. Racism is first and foremost about power. It determines who gets what, when, and how much. The effective external realities of racism surround us everyday; it is so pervasive that it affects every aspect of our lives, however much of it goes unrecognized. Witness the harassment of African-American shoppers, in downtown stores throughout America; the redlining of African people's community by banks as a device for denying access to loans; although less than previously, lest we forget the old American custom - cross burning on the lawns of African-American homeowners, the bombings of home and churches, cut down by a sniper on a dark country road, or sometimes in broad daylight in front of a court house. We had our last old fashion public lynching of Michael Donald in Mobil, Alabama as recent as 1981. Racism is a public evil, which causes private pain.

Understanding Racism as an Ideology

The attempt to define the justified, indignant and correct reaction of African people to "white supremacy" as "Black" racism is in effect a dishonest and deceitful expression to disguise the maintenance of "white supremacy". Such unfounded claims are yet another attempt to distort the righteous, historical and noble struggle of African-Americans for true liberation, from the legacy of the past. The institution of enslavement ended just about 150 years, a little over three generations ago. Racism is not absolutely, but is essentially an institutional phenomenon. It is prejudice plus power. And it is initiated and carried out primarily by the powerful who control the major resources in this republic. The basic tenets of racism are aggression, domination, and greed; like the air, it permeates the entire Republic. Even billionaire Oprah Winfrey is not immune to this virus. Racism does not react. Racism as an agent of aggression and itself manifests overtly (racial profiling or Stop and Frisk) or covertly (redlining by financial institutions). It acts - almost everywhere, almost all the time.

Racism was not born in America. It was brought here. The idea had been initiated and well honed among Europeans themselves, as a collection of "races", Nordics, Alpine, Celts, etc. This was broadened to include more people with contrasting looks during the exploration period. Practices evolved from the idea of "race" with the rise of the modern West. To define racism as "white supremacy" does not mean that white people, in the generality, are bad apples. Most white people are not mean. But some of them are. White supremacy can't be traced to an individual psychological disorder, because it is inherent in the prevailing social order. And too often they are in high places. I am now speaking here again of a doctrine, an ideology, a system of ideas, a body of beliefs, predictable values and customs, unfair legal practices that dominate the thinking of the courts and police departments and lawyers. The big ideas are always controlled and propagated, by elites wherever they rule. Racism can be looked at in the same way that Communism once functioned in the former Soviet Union. Communism was run by elites, by bureaucrats, as was Nazi Germany, as was Apartheid in the Republic of South Africa, as was the American south, by the landed gentry – the first segregationist, or the rising pre bellum capitalist class in the north. Action is shaped by ideology. The fact that most people in the Soviet Union were not card holding members (less than 1 in 10 of the total population) of the Communist party is less relevant than the fact that the population living under a system that was dominated by Communists, and that this system controlled their very lives through the control of major institutions, or the cultural apparatus, which controlled their collective minds. The people in power orchestrated this ideology to serve their ends, i.e. the ideals of Communism. Similarly, in America, the ideology is based on the doctrine of "white supremacy". Whether legal or de facto, whether malignant or benign, the ideas propounded by the system of white supremacy prevail. Due to a long history of custom, habits, values, mores, ingrained beliefs, which evolve into norms. Thus "white supremacy" has acquired a life of its own. Custom is more powerful than the force of written law. Habits and social convention influence individual attitudes. A collective outlook, a collective myth, produces collective patterns of behavior. The wisdom, moral clarity, grace, and pure common sense of the honorable Nelson Mandela teaches us "No one is born hating another person because of the color of his skin, or his background, or his religion."

"Race" is the Principle, Racism the Act

The root and reality of racism grows out of the fallacies concept of "race." We do not seem to realize how recent this concept of people belonging to "races" is. It has not been much more than three centuries that the term "race" itself in reference to humans gained traction the English language. This idea was imposed on conquered "colored peoples" throughout the world. "Race" as we currently carry such a notion in our heads, is largely a myth, a fiction or a stage of false consciousness. The construction of "race" does not correspond to reality, however much we think it does. Categories of "races" exist, but races do not. "Race" is a superstition, our modem-day witchcraft. As a function, racism is also a political principle. It has generated an effective political culture among people who unwittingly accepts whiteness or the classification of "white". Being "white" is not a color. It is a state of mind. It's even a moral choice. It is an idea that belongs to our epoch, our period of time. Just as the Greeks during their epoch, believed non-Greeks were barbarous, uncivilized, savages. They praised not one, but many Gods. We believe in "race", which reigns with God-like power over our lives. This doctrine begins with, but does not end with so called "white" people. All people, of all colors are effected by this doctrine. Certain Black Americans can be effective agents of this doctrine. Blacks, too often see other Blacks through the eyes of white people. Long ago in *The Souls of Black Folks*, W.E.B. Dubois described this phenomenon, "It is a peculiar sensation, this double-consciousness, this sense of always looking at one's self through the eyes of others."

The error in "race thinking" is that we are taught to believe that there is an intrinsic link between biology and what is essentially social. We have been taught to believe that physical traits have an intrinsic connection to all behavior. We believe that "race" has some fixed, immutable tie to individual ability and cultural achievement. From this erroneous concept of "race" we arrive at a set of assumptions about the natural superiority of one "race" over others. We are taught this belief from our formal school curricula. The American system of education is a submission to the doctrine of white supremacy. No thoughtful human being will deny this fact. Careful examination reveals that this "natural superiority" has more to do with environment, nurturing, and the fortuitous turns of history, not to mention the force of arms, and a system of suppression than with genes or "pure" bloodlines.

It borders on obscenity that we live in a world of marvelous material advances, and at the same time remain bound to the obsolete and dangerous idea of "race" formed during the era of ignorance, superstition, and pseudo-science. To be sure all people are creatures of habits and preservers of tradition. This accounts, in part, for the maintenance of this doctrine. The idea of "race" evolved rather gradually and uncertainly during the great geographic "discoveries" along with the "discovery" of the great variety of humanity, not to mention great fortunes in the 15th and 16th centuries. It was then that this powerful "modern myth" took root. The widespread beliefs that we hold about "race" can be traced to the rise of this dynamic, and to the creation of modern Western Europe. There is no other real index that we can point to. Almost all of the concepts, both "scientifically" and mythically, that we know about "race" is derived from European languages, thought, and through widespread conquests, imperialism and empire building. This glaring, experiential fact would be difficult for any rational person to deny. The die has been cast. And here we are. The words/categories of Negro, mulattos, quadroons, octoroons, mestizo, griffy, half-breed, or Indian, as in American Indian, were all derived from European languages. All categories of "race" as we know them can't be divorced from the European-Judeo-Christian world.

Some Historical References

Let us briefly examine the evolution of the idea of "race". Like so many words, concepts, and ideas the term "race" has obscure origins. It has been variously cited as deriving from the Arabic word, *Ras*; or the Latin word, *Ratio*, which means *order* or *root*. Another Latin word, *Raza*, has also been shown to have some etymological connection to the word "race." In the modern languages of Spanish and Portuguese, which are derived from Vulgar Latin, it is connected to the word *Raza* (root).

According to the very distinguished anthropologist Ashley Montagu, the first use of the word "race" printed in the English language is to be found in the second edition of martyrologist John Foxe's *Acts and Monuments*, popularly known as *The Book of Martyrs*, published in 1570. In this work the author writes, "Thus was the outward "race" stock of Abraham after flesh refused…" - a rather special use of the term referring to family, offspring, posterity, or person. In the sense of a tribe, nation, or people descended from common stock, the first English usage of the term is to be found in Wynne's *History of the Gwyder Family*, published in 1600, where the author refers to Llewelyn Griffith as "the last prince of Wales of the British race".

In the sense of a breed or stock of animals or a particular variety of a species, the first English usage occurs in Blundeville's *Horsemanship*, published in 1580. In the sense of one of the major groups of humankind having certain physical traits in common, the English usage occurs in Oliver Goldsmith's *The Natural History of Animals*, which appeared in 1774, and in which he writes, "The second great variety in the human species seems to be that of Tar Tar race." In France, Francois Taut, in his book entitled *Tresor de la langue francais*, published in 1600, "race" is derived from the word *raddit* and stated that it "alludes to the extraction of a man, of a dog, of a horse, as one says of a good 'race'."

The foregoing is but a capsule, and yet I think, useful impression of the derivation of the word "race". As an idea it is shrouded in a crazy quilt pattern of connotations, which finally settles as a loose, but popular definition of the divisions among humankind. It is inexact, fluid, abstract, scarcely concrete, and yet today "race" is a word whose emotive power and quality of meaning invokes impressions of a holy writ. It is a word and an idea, most certainly in the modern world, that has caused far more confusion, public, private, and political pain, than any social construction devised by the human mind. Dr. Montagu has called the idea of "race" a fallacy, and "man's most dangerous myth." It is my contention that the modern idea of "race" has generated more unmerited suffering than any single system that underlies political and economic oppression.

The Rise of Scientific Racism

In less than 300 years, "race" has become a part of the ideological underpinnings of the Western world. Many of its most articulate exponents, ironically enough, are companions to the rise of modern science. The so-called "natural philosophers" ran the first leg in advancement of this dangerous idea. It was, to begin with, a somewhat innocent method and interpretation of what science does: categorize, catalogue, inventory, describe, and analyze. Names like Gregor Mendel and Carl Linnaeus represented a rather apolitical and innocent curiosity about "race" during the Age of Enlightenment in the late l8th and early 19th centuries. There were others to follow, who made the idea of "race" central to their pseudoscientific thinking that coincided with the powers of conquest of so-called "inferior races". The writing of the German instigator Johann Blumenbach introduces the word "Caucasian" to the lexicon for the first time in 1795. By the early 19th century a plethora of "race" thinkers, writers, and prophets emerged. It was they who did so much to advance this modern world paradigm about "race". Georges-Louis Leclerc, Comte de Buffon, the Frenchman, Johann Friedrich Blumenbach, the German, Joseph Arthur Comte de Gobineau, the Frenchman, and Houston Stewart Chamberlain, the British-born turned German National, spiritual and intellectual father of Adolf Hitler are examples of the sinister minds that assured that "white race supremacy" and master "race" theories would be the order of the day. By the end of the 18th century systems of government arranged by European Imperialism, in India and other parts of Asia, and the earlier settler states of South Africa, Australia, New Zealand, Latin America, and North America, (all before Nazi Germany) were established throughout the world, east and west. Thus, racist ideas become dominant themes in western European relations with the rest of the world. The "white man" as Europeans collectively presented themselves, were suddenly surrounded by "inferior races". It was the "white man's burden" in India, and "manifest destiny" in America. This new "race" ideology is primarily responsible for the legal structures and social policies that we know as Jim Crow, segregation, apartheid, or by extension, the Nuremberg laws. It is responsible for the gaggle of absurdities that negate, stifle, and pervert human personality by twisting biology into half-breeds, mulattos, quadroons, octoroons, griffys, and being mixed-race or "tawny-stained", as opposed to being "pure white".

Beginning some 90 years ago, with a new school of scientific thinkers spearheaded by anthropologists such as Franz Boas of Columbia University, Melville Herskovitz of Northwestern University, and later, a student of Boas, Ruth Benedict, the idea of "race" and the myth erected around laws was challenged. And thanks to their work, today "race" as a scientific concept has been mostly abandoned. According to Leonard Lieberman, professor of anthropology at Central Michigan University, the concept of "race" is now undergoing deconstruction. The majority of anthropologists no longer support the "race" concept. Dr. Lieberman, anthropologist stated, " 'Race' is more than half toward rejection and disposition."

Why "Race" is a False Concept

The first thing that is wrong with the idea of "race" (in this scientific age) is that it violates the basic laws of science, which ironically gave this idea its false birth. The first laws of science are observation and consistency. The scientific mode begins with what is consistent with what we observe. Evidence must be based on what is empirical, according to the laws of science. That is to say, it is observation and experience (empirical, proven evidence) that determines what is a scientific truth. Now it is obvious to the naked eye that there is no such thing as "race" in the sense that we carry this dangerous idea in our heads, which suggests we are bound to some uniform genetic code that causes people who look alike to behave alike, to think, know and feel and even believe alike. While specific groups of people who share very similar physical traits do behave alike, this bio-social factor is emphatically not determined solely by genes. Within the populations that we define as "races", white, black, yellow, etc. there are a range of looks and behaviors that defies the notion of "uniform, unspoiled sameness". People who share common physical traits, i.e. hair, facial and body types, color, and eye fold do not conform to some pure and absolute physical presence. This can be viewed by the naked eye. People who have been isolated from other people by geographic separation over many centuries will acquire a general set of common physical, as well as common behavioral characteristics because of isolation, inbreeding, and mutation. This process is a result of nature and environment, and not simply genes. People who are members of the same immediate families tend to look more alike in contrast to other families.

The racists who promote the idea of a pure "race" based on skin color or other obvious physical traits in common, are a recent phenomenon in human history and are clearly a product of the modern world. The identity of peoplehood has heretofore revolved around language, land, religion, or some profound myth in their backgrounds and not on such a superficial thing as skin color and still does today.

The myth of "race" as we claim its meaning in America can be quite simply exposed by examining the peoples of the world today. Despite about 300 years of enduring some fiercely consistent propaganda about "race", Western Europeans, or "white" people, if you like, the peoplehoods of Europe are still bound by language, beliefs, deep-rooted myths, geography, and religion. There is no continent on Earth in which all the people behave the "same" because of their color or some other conspicuous physical trait. Europeans themselves represent one of the best examples that there is no such thing as an immutable fixture of "races", or that solidarity, politically or otherwise, is inspired solely by "race." Witness the 1,000 years of incessant conflict among "white" people (before they became "white") from the fall of Rome to the rise of Hitler's Third Reich in Germany. If "race" causes sameness in thought and action, beliefs and values, feelings and imagination, how do we explain the centuries of conflict among "yellow" people in Asia, Black people in Africa, and the indigenous, or so-called "red" people in the Americas? It can be argued that more often than not, conflict has been intra-racial for a much longer period of time than interracial. The nemeses of Europeans have been other Europeans from the Jutes, Picts, the Anglos, Saxons, Vandals, Normans, Prussians, Barbarians, Serbs and Croates ad infinitum. None of these peoples called themselves "white" in the way that we use the term today. They were not "white" yet. There was no "super white race". History had to produce them as one "super white tribe". The nemeses of Asians have been other Asians since time immemorial. Over time the Japanese have inflicted more harm on other Asians than any other geographic populations or "races" of the world. The Zulus under the rage of Shaka, though not great in size and scope, represents one of the most compelling examples of African on African bloodletting, in what is now called the Republic of South Africa.

Despite the facts, as well as the truth of history, the myth of "races" by color delineation, or other physical traits still holds a powerful grip on the contemporary human mind. There is the saying that people get what they want because they want what they get. The belief in the myth, indeed, the modern superstition of "race" is just such a proposition. This belief is easily one of the most exploitable ideas causing people to emphasize their differences, which they have scarcely taken time to think about clearly. In this modern, scientific, super-charged world of the magic of technology, we are trapped by ignorance, habit, fallacy, fear, superstition, and a modern ideology that manipulates our actions; sow seeds of hatred, ill will, and distrust.

Reductio ad Absurdum, or The Absurdity of "Race" as the Logic of Power

Even while it holds a vice-like dominance over much of the modern mind, the superstition of "race" remains one the most confused ideas in the whole history of ideas. "Race" is something every American seems to know without thinking about it. Few people can talk "race" with definite clarity. The exception to this general rule would be those practitioners who are consciously committed to "white supremacy" or, "master race" Aryan values. Their belief about "race" is central to their identity. To them, the meaning of "race" claims some sort of purity; a pure undiluted genetic stock. This belief is so profound that at both the conscious, as well as the unconscious level, it functions as a religion. Conventional wisdom claims that religion deals with God, or the supreme power - the being to which human beings owe their highest loyalty everywhere. "Race" and "race thinking" supersedes God in the everyday world of the racist. In effect, the belief in the idea of "race" and the practice of racism is a secular religion, far more powerful in exercising control of behavior than the religion of Christianity regardless of denomination. Case in point: after the Civil Rights Movement's successful dismantling of formal school segregation, there emerged a lively movement to establish "Christian schools" throughout the South. Coincidentally, these "Christian schools" were all "white". No African people were allowed in such Christian schools. By the late 1960s in the state of Mississippi, more than half of the "white" students left the public schools for "private Christian schools". Which claims the brotherhood of man - Christian religion or "race"?

"Race" indoctrination, in fact, absorbs and perverts the biblical stories and arranges them to support the "white superiority" and "Black inferiority" paradigm. There were at least 44 rationales drawn from the Holy Bible to justify the institution of "Negro Slavery". "The Curse of Ham" is the best known of the long litany of curses "imposed" on African people by God. "The Curse of Ham" says that people with very dark skin should "forever be the servant of man" (meaning "white" man). According to racist interpretation of the Bible, certain characters who violated the laws of God were to be punished perpetually. Ham, who laughed at the naked body of his father Noah; Cain who murdered his brother Abel; and Haggar, who boar a child for Abraham, the husband of Sarah, were all black-skinned people, and thus, sinners against God Almighty. This is called demonizing. This is what caused Whitaker Chambers, the intellectual, to define Black people as the "most God-obsessed and man-despised people on the face of the earth." Brilliant though he was, Whitaker Chambers didn't know the first thing about all the people of the earth. Think about African people who are quite diverse and quite old.

It is never quite explained by racist Christian preachers, who support this doctrine, what must have been the color of the other family members of Ham. If Ham was Black, then what color were his brothers Shem and Jepheth, not to mention his father Noah? Was Ham Black before or after "The Curse"? What color was Abel, Cain's brother, who was "the first murder victim" in the world? Maybe this family was an interracial family? These are just a few examples of racial absurdities imposed on the Bible retroactively. Historians call this "presentism", wherein you define the past by the present without qualification. The idea of "race", as we understand the concept, is a distinctively modern idea. The categories that we use, not to mention the context that we live in, were not a part of the ancient world. "Negroes" did not exist in the Bible. Ethiopians did. It should not be surprising that Puritans of New England, such as Cotton Mather, believed in such a doctrine, as do the present day Calvinists of the South African Dutch Reform Church and their belief in predestination. Joseph Smith, the founder of the Latter Day Saints, or the Mormons as this faith is commonly known, subscribed to this doctrine when he got his tablet of laws, like Moses, from God in America in 1830 through his angel Moroni. The dispensation of the Mormons' belief that black-skinned people were cursed has just been renounced within the past few years. Someone has suggested that the ban on a limited African-American participation in the Mormon faith was lifted not so much because of a new dispensation from God, but the definite need for a few swift Black halfbacks; leaping wide receivers, and a rugged linebacker or two, to play on the Brigham Young University football team. The Mormons, too, have learned that "you can't win without 'em". A curious note is that the Mormons did not apply the color bar to dark-skinned people everywhere. Among black-skinned people in the South Pacific this "colorism" was not intact. Only to Black people in America did the Mormons insist that Black skin was a "curse". This fact suggests the special need to use "race" as a tool to disempower Black people within the body politic of the United States. Mormons or Later Day-Saints is an expressly American religion. Joseph Smith found his faith in the midst of the firery furnace of a nation that long ago religiously bowed down to the muscular doctrine of white, over Black, supremacy.

The key to understanding the function of racism in American life is that it is fused into the national ethos. Religion, American nationalism, or patriotism - American values all mean the same thing - Europeans (or better still – "white" people) should rule. The purity of "race" gives a right to monopolize power, and indeed, the right to exploit others economically, politically, socially, and culturally with impunity. In some form "race" is at the heart of the power struggle in the Americas, South Africa, or wherever else this "race" factor can be used against non-Europeans. At bottom, power has little to do with who is the majority in a given society. Power is exercised by power majorities, who may be numerical minorities such as in the country of South Africa. This is how imperialism and colonialism have been exercised throughout the world - by numerical minorities who were power majorities. At bottom, the emergence of the idea of "race" in the modem world is inseparable from the uses of power - how it is harnessed, shared, or denied. The belief in "race" has no other significant or useful value other than being the pivot around which power turns. Power is associated with skin color and all that it implies, the major indicator of "race" (i.e. "white" over Black). Many people in this world have come to accept such an image as a normal part of reality, something that is, as if by nature. This is despite the fact that we see power struggles all over the world - in Northern Ireland, Eastern Europe, the former Soviet Union, among so-called "white" people. From this we can see that "race" alone does not dictate solidarity among peoples, as we are taught here in the United States. Nothing more graphically illustrates the myth of "race" than the incessant acts of genocide among "white" people in Eastern Europe, or Germany during the Nazi reign. No "tribes" in Africa can match the bloodletting that we witness among "the white race" in Europe. Such infighting in Africa would be called "Black on Black" violence, which is another sinister manipulation of the idea of "race". Black people are stigmatized by "race", meaning Blacks are "race" ridden, whites are not. Whites are the pristine "race". In certain cases violence becomes more a color than an act. In Europe it's Serbs opposing Croats, Czechs opposing Slovaks, Georgians fighting Russians and not "white on white violence". Why? Fact: a people or ethnic group is not a "race". In a situation where rulers can tie in conspicuous physical traits (such as color) to power sharing, they have done so - in the United States, South Africa, New Zealand, Australia, Latin America, India, and the Islands of the Sea, "race" is a most convenient political tool to divide and rule humanity. The belief in "race" may be an absurdity, but when connected to the desire and ability to exercise power, in Machiavellian terms, it is perfectly logical, however immoral, primitive, destructive, and mad.

Perhaps the most overlooked reality of racist attitudes is how it so often causes otherwise intelligent people to behave rather stupidly. Mere casual observation of such behavior reveals how powerful the influence of the doctrine is. People who are enslaved to the values of racism may feel, say, or do anything that appears absurd and ridiculous when viewed in the light of human reason.

"All 'Negroes' look alike," how utterly simple-minded. Have such people ever looked at "Negroes"? Do they see with their eyes? Of course not! They see with their beliefs, which distort their minds, feelings, etc. What this means is that they want all "Negroes" to look alike. They make it easy to ignore the great variety of colors, hair forms, and facial contours. Many of the "Negroes" look almost exactly like the late Negrophobe J. Edgar Hoover of the FBI. Therein lies the problem. Do "Negroes" sometimes look "white" because of artificial insemination or human co-habitation? This is a part of what Baldwin calls "the unspeakable".

According to racist logic, all behavior can be attributed to "race". Individual ability or cultural achievement is accounted for by "race". African people are supposed to be more criminally inclined, less likely to value education, seek employment, care for their families; more prone to lie, cheat, or steal than Europeans - simply because of their "race". Black people are, in effect, less endowed to be decent human beings than "whites". The cause of this uneven distribution of positive traits comes from one or two sources: religion (i.e. arranged by God Almighty) and nature, which is less generous to African people in the endowments of intelligence and talent. Since the 19th century, this can be proven by "science". Any reasonable observation can dispel the falsehood of such beliefs; nevertheless they persist. Again the idea of "race" was imposed on religion first, then science.

A glaring and gruesome fact, such as the monotonous and senseless murder of Black people by "whites" over many generations, does not stigmatize "whites" as violent. Power is responsible for obscuring this reality. More than half the people in death row are Black men and women. Until very recently, no "white" person had ever received the death sentence for taking the life of a Black person in the whole history of capital punishment in the United States. Power arranges this obscenity. There is a clear-cut connection between "race" and power. The crazy quilt - contradictory, tragic, and oft absurd behavior on the part of American people generated by the idea of "race", is the premise from which logic flows. A simple syllogism explains it all: All Black people steal from downtown stores. The multilingual, super educated medical doctor, Dr. Charles Hawkins is Black, and therefore, Dr. Hawkins will steal from downtown stores. "Race" is a false premise that promotes faulty logic, and absurd conclusions. At bottom, such logic is legitimized by power.

VIGNETTES FROM THE WORLD OF RACISM

The Drinking Fountain: Segregate the Water, and Maybe the Air

One of the most graphic symbols of southern Jim Crow law was the legal establishment of separate drinking fountains for "white" and "colored". This is a sad commentary on how utterly stupid grown people can be. This artificial arrangement was enough to convince "white" people that they were inherently better than Africans. How fragile. How easily fooled into a false sense of superiority. The water came from the same treatment plant, flowed through the same pipelines to the mouths of people, "white" and Black. Designating separate water fountains according to "race" made perfectly, good sense to these retarded, southern political leaders and their unthinking, submissive, lock-step constituencies of the South. There is little doubt here that the energy put into such laws accounts, in part, for the social backwardness of southern "whites" to this very day. Though Black people were humiliated by

Jim Crow, they were less affected. They were not made into nincompoops. They knew it was stupid. They knew that they were human beings, white were not sure.

God Made Us Do It: The Misuse of the Holy Bible

Misinterpretation and misapplication of the Biblical text has been central in the rise of "race" thinking. Distortion and out - of - context readings were used to sanction slavery. Clergy, and lay people alike, twisted the Scripture. The Bible became a device that placed "white" people close to God while African people, who were to be used for brutish labor, were placed beyond the pale of salvation. The venom of racism was manifest in many trial courts of the South when up until the 1960's "whites" and African people had to be sworn in on separate Bibles. There was apparently something awful about Black people that contaminated "whites" - except when raising their children, cooking their food, and nursing the whole family. It was James Baldwin who proclaimed that the Black mammy on southern plantations and there after was the world's first psychiatrist long before Sigmund Freud. It was she who listened to the social-emotional problems and dispensed advice and comfort to each member of the dysfunctional slave holding family.

The Restaurant: Keep the Niggers Out!

Among the many absurdities generated by formal racial segregation was the denial of the simple right of African people to be served in public restaurants. The managers of such establishments, in the South especially, would routinely spare no ends to prevent close physical proximity between Black and "white" people. For "white" and Black people to eat from the same lunch counter was an abomination, which violated the highest codes of racial etiquette. Few things could be more offensive to "white" southern sensibilities than eating in a public place with Black people. One of the most celebrated occasions in the struggle to break segregation involved a future governor in the early 1960s.

Lester Maddox, the owner of Pickwick Restaurant in Atlanta, Georgia gave his "white" customers ax handles with which to beat up Black people who attempted to "integrate" his restaurant. During this episode Mr. Maddox was predictably stupid. He was perfectly willing to allow Black people to cook the food - sweaty palms and all - that went into pristine stomachs of "white" folks. Maddox was a superbly stupid man, yet he was elected to the State of Georgia's highest office.

Unity Without Uniformity: Competitive Stupidity

During the heyday of segregation, the several southern, border, and indeed, northern states were in fierce competition to "out-stupid" one another. Mindless meanness was the order of the day. A general spirit captured the racist mentality. In some deep southern states Black people entered the front of the bus, paid their fares, and then went to the back of the bus to take a seat. In some other deep southern states Black people entered the front of the bus, paid their fares, promptly exited, and re-entered the bus through the back door to take their seats in the back of the bus. From this, one can surmise that some states were more "liberal" than others. In some states, in some retail stores Black people were literally not allowed to try on clothes, or fit a hat before they bought them. In other states there would sometimes be a hired Black clerk to accommodate Black customers, where clothes were set aside that could be tried on. It was almost universal that Africans who went to downtown theaters in southern cities were confined to the balcony. Blacks saw better from up high, one supposes. At spectator sporting events - football, baseball, and basketball games to be precise - there was the proverbial "rope" that separated Black people from "white" people and at public beaches, the same thing. One incredible incongruity that slapped legal segregation down was "Negro music". It was not uncommon in the segregated South, long before integration, for young "white" people to show up for all Black dances or stage shows with a space reserved for them, and not at their insistence. The police were always there to keep people in the proper place. The proverbial "rope" was there to keep the "races" from mixing. But invariably the music, that irresistible, magical mad stuff that Black people seem to create so effortlessly, would cause the "whites" to disregard the "rope", give Jim Crow a swift kick in the pants, and come over to the Black side and try to swing. This played havoc with the policeman, who never quite knew what to do about it but look with a wish that he had the nerve to do likewise, and be so human.

Segregation Up South

It is a misnomer to believe that segregation of "the races" was confined only to rebel states. Segregation in America was (and is) a universal reality. Forms and style differ, but the essence of racism remains the same. Northern segregation is called *de facto* segregation in legal language. This means that customs, beliefs, deep-seated values prevailed over the laws on the books. Throughout the north for most of the 20th century there was no legal basis for segregation, but it happened anyway. Bert Williams, the great Black comedian who actually wore "black face" as the star of the Ziegfeld Follies on Broadway during the 1920s, always entered the theater through the freight elevator to get to the stage so that "white" audiences could greet him with the adulation and thunderous applause. Paul Robeson, the greatest of the suppressed names of great Americans, frequently ran into problems getting accommodations at hotels, even in liberal New York, where he was starring in the role of Othello, the longest running Shakespearean play in the history of Broadway. Racism is learned ignorance. It is not quite stupidity. Ignorance can be fixed, but stupidity is forever. Racism can be modified, sometimes changed, and other times arrested to keep its aggression in check.

School for the Truly Blind

The well-known "genius" of soul music, Ray Charles, tells of a tragi-comic experience that he witnessed and endured as an innocent child. After losing his sight at the age of six or seven or so, he was enrolled by his mother into the school for the blind in St. Augustine, Florida. Of all things that happened while attending this school, he held an outstanding recollection of one thing: the children of the school were rigidly segregated on the basis of "race". Great pains were taken by the authorities to obey the segregated manmade laws of the state to keep "white" and Black children separate from one another in every aspect of life. They were together, but separate and through it all, the children remained blind. Despite the fact the children could not even see the world that surrounded them, the authorities acted as if they could.

Higher Learning According to God

In the state of South Carolina there is a full-fledged, solidly accredited college known as Bob Jones University. The founder, Bob Jones himself, claims Biblical inspiration for the establishment of the well-respected institution. It is what is called a fundamentalist learning center that is connected to the mystical body of Christ. Surprisingly, and inexplicably, the student body included African Americans. The policy of the school does not deny matriculation on the basis of "race". Policy does, however, state that "interracial" dating is taboo. Blacks and "whites" of the opposite sex can be suspended if caught in intimate association with one another. "The Curse of Ham" has not been lost on the theological foundation of this Christian institution. What we have here is idiocy multiplied by 10. This leads us to some famous last words: "I know what you want, you want to marry my daughter." And the antidote to this scornful declaration is this: "No, I do not want to marry your daughter - knowing the family as I do."

Afterword

Over the past several centuries the idea of "race" and the reality of racism has emerged in our world, and as a consequence, has produced the most frightful horror stories known to humankind. Unearned suffering is the stuff of this phenomenon that we have come to call racism. The bottomless brutalization leading to enslavement, land dispossession, and conscious acts of mass murder that we know as genocide, are all rooted in the belief in "race" and the practice of racism.

All of the relevant facts, ideas, concrete acts, and covert deeds are well documented; the capture and enslavement of untold millions of Africans, and the conquest of and genocidal practices against the indigenous peoples of the Americas and the islands of seas, in combination, represent the largest example of human devastation that this world has ever witnessed. The "Black man" and the "red man" viewed as "inferior races" spawned an incredible absence of human sentiment. Powerful forces that adopted the modern world idea of "race" as a creed effectively violated the most sacred codes of Judeo-Christian ethics. Later in history, though far less massive in scope, but no less in degree of cruelty, was decimation of millions of European Jews and other "races" in the movement to cleanse Europe of undesirables in affecting the purity of the "Aryan master race". The Holocaust produced by mad scientists of The Third Reich is a lesson in human degradation that is finally becoming a part of the moral history of the world. "Race" thinking is singularly responsible for lesser known episodes in "man's inhumanity to man", genocide in Tasmania, Australia, and King Leopold's Congo; and the killing fields in the former Yugoslavia between the Serbs, Croats, ad Muslims. "Ethnic cleansing" functions as a definition of "race". The fact that such people would normally belong to the "white race" is irrelevant. The idea of "race" can be imposed on anyone according to myth, superstition, or law. "Race" thinking can be applied, practiced and edified by any group and any gender. Sigmund Freud's celebrated statement that "anatomy is destiny" or one's gender or "race" determines one's main personality traits is a type of "race" thinking. Thus, based on a person's gender, or "race" one can dictate/predict their role and place in society. The anatomy or physical trait can lead to whether or not a woman can drive a bus.

Anything human made can be unmade by humankind. The categories and classifications of "race" were brought to religion and science, not the other way around. Again "race" is an invention, not a discovery. "Race" is an invention of the mind, as are all ideas. It was invented in a time and context when people were much less aware of themselves than they are now. In the over 200 years since census first came about in the United States, 26 racial categories have been used. Since then, the government has found a new way to classify its people in virtually every decade. The two most notable categories '"white" and "Negro/Black" have been taken apart from time to time. For instance, in 1890 the census takers were careful to make distinctions between "Blacks", "mulattos", "quadroons", and "octoroons". In the 1920 census, the categories were reduced to "Negro" and "mulatto". In today's world all of these people are classified as Black. In 1930, nine classifications of "race" were on the census: "White", "Negro", Mexican, Indian, Chinese, Japanese, Filipino, Hindu, and Korean. In 1940 the Mexican classification was gone. Today the American population fits into five categories: White, Black or African American, American Indian or Alaska Native, Asian, Native Hawaiian or Other Pacific Islander. In addition, "race" and ethnicity are considered separate and distinct identities, with Hispanic or Latino origin asked as a separate question. All of the "race" categories are artificial, and the definitions are arbitrary. It is self-evident that "race" is an obsolete idea. Each generation must make life anew. At this hour, we are now challenged to make life anew.

What has been done, can be undone, as regards to categories of "race". The challenge is to liberate ourselves from this vocabulary, "which cannot bear the weight of the reality" that we are living. Human beings are the only animals in the kingdom who are capable of defining themselves and the world in which they live. Human identity is a constant struggle in the ongoing evolution of the species. "Race" as a concept, as an idea and a way to declare one's "who-ness" is clearly inadequate and obsolete. Who people are, as opposed to what they look like, is more significantly a function of environment and experience - that is to say, using history and culture, other than simple, observable biological traits. The color of skin, shape of the nose, and the form of hair, does not determine who people are. The first step to repudiating "race" is to place this myth before the bar of public discourse; place it in school curriculum for purpose of analysis, and demand from political leaders, legal categories that respect the background of people as shaped by their true heritage - cultural and social heritage. Everything changes, all the time. We can help to shape change, or let change shape us. What we lack is what we must discover - and that is moral clarity.

"Race" is a Myth - Racism is a Reality

Some misconceptions about "race": 1) that there is a unity between physical, mental, social, and personal traits; 2) that "race" makes for inborn traits that are immutable, fixed by laws of nature. Dr. Ashley Montagu has defined "race" as a "Fallacy," which has become "Man's Most Dangerous Myth."

Statements on Race: The Myth

"Race" is an invention and not a discovery:

People representing different physical types, while occupying the same social space is as old as societies beyond the state of tribalism. Differences are not new, it is our conception of difference that is new.

"Race" is an intellectual construction:

The idea of "race" is in part a product of human imagination. The intellectual, with his/her penchant for categorizing, cataloging, and pigeonholing life is the author of the idea of "race". People in the academies (16 and 17 centuries) gave "race" its content. As such, "race" is an idea that does not correspond to reality. "Race" is an idea that belongs solely to the modem world.

"Race" as an idea is unscientific, because it violates the first laws of science, which are observation and consistency:

"Race" thinking is a product of social beliefs that have emerged around "race" outside of scientific findings about "race". Science properly defines "races" as "geographic populations" which are subject to mutation. "Races" are not stagnant phenomena in the way that such appears in our muddled and popular imagination.

Categories of "races" exist, but "races" do not:

Science seeks to categorize "races" based on material particles that are inherited (genes) which are responsible for the way people look as to physical types. Science does not contend that there is an intrinsic link to biology and behavior. "Races" exist in our minds' eye according to our beliefs and cultural mythology. The belief in "race" is nothing more than a superstition.

Statements on Racism: The Reality

Racism is based on doctrine, a belief system, an ideology, a whole system of ideas - it is more than a question of people simply not liking each other as individuals because they are different. It is because of the symbols and cultural values. The doctrine of racism has varied through time and space, but the essence of racism remains the same. It is based on domination and exploitation of a group that believes it is superior and its subordination of another group and inequitable relations between the two. Modern western European colonialism, America's slavery, the Nazi movement in Germany, Apartheid in South Africa, segregation in Australia and New Zealand are all based on "race" or white supremacist doctrines, supported by institutions, myths, customs, mores, habits, and religious beliefs.

Racism is largely an institutional phenomenon - legally, politically, economically, socially, culturally, religiously. Institutional power represents the greatest expression of racism and not individual isolated acts of racism. Racism has systemic expression. Laws, policies, and regulations out of a structural framework manifestly patent it. Control of power and resources are expressed institutionally, i.e. the ability to control the actions of men and women by making or enforcing certain policies, granting or withholding economic opportunity and controlling sources of information.

Racism also has life of its own beyond institutions. It is cultural phenomenon found in small habits, nuances, and traits, such traits as small as the way a racist would shake ones hand. Interpersonal contact with people who are different can be a horrifying experience for the practitioner of racism.

Racism is based on aggression domination and greed. Racism sanctions the right of exploitation by one group over another. Most racism is practiced covertly, (i.e. under disguise, covered, concealed secret) and not overt (i.e. open, public, manifest, and not concealed, secret, and hidden).

A Working Definition of Culture

The definition of a culture is the definition of a people. Culture represents the collective experiences of human thought, human will, and human action. We feel safe in asserting that every people possess culture. A culture is a way of life. There are no groups of people with a long history together who are deprived of culture unless they are, as individuals, dead. Every single individual is a creature of some culture. We find that culture is expressed in many ways. Culture is, on the one hand, particular, special, or different, and on the other hand, it is universal, and quite similar as a function.

That is to say, culture is the basis of understanding distinct differences among groups of people, one from the other, as well as a basis for understanding commonalities that people have, i.e. family, religion, governance and politics. Culture indeed, on a worldwide scale, manifests a unity of opposites; this unity is based on certain basic human arrangements that must be met in order for people to live as social beings. And yet people structure their lives in different ways to meet their basic needs. People in Africa, Asia, and the Americas behaved differently before the coming of the peoples from Western Europe. They represent different geographic, physical, biological, and social worlds, which constitute their respective ecologies, wherein they develop the ways to meet the elements within their surroundings.

A culture responds to what is demanded of it. We should not expect Eskimos to build skyscrapers.

Culture is not biological, although some aspect of biology may influence it. Genes cannot transmit it. Blue eyes do not determine what language one will speak. Dark skin does not determine whether one is a Jew, Christian, Muslim, a Buddhist, or Zoroastrianism - culture does. Nobody, in actuality, is born with religion, or for that matter, good rhythm. Like mannerisms, gestures, and other aspects of motor behavior, rhythm is taught. It is taught to individuals by habits that are inherent in the culture, from a people's pattern of behavior. Every culture has a rhythm of it's own.

Culture is transmitted through enduring processes commonly called institutions. Institutions are the most direct manifestations of organized living arrangements. It is through institutions, working collectively and interdependently, that culture molds and shapes our lives towards cooperative intelligence and group solidarity. Culture, then, is handed down from one generation to another and represents the core values of individuals that are learned, shaped, and shared by the total group experience, past and present: Language, religion, family, art, mores, folkways, customs, habits, laws, myths, emotions, gestures, material and non-material creations are all a part of that complex whole, that makes up the stuff of culture.

Culture is not a distinctively individual phenomenon. It is a group phenomenon. Individuals do not invent culture by themselves they contribute to it. They inherit it socially from the group. In a real sense each individual is a creature of his/her culture.

Culture does not belong to any group, according to age or sex, so long as age and sex groups possess the same fundamental history of experiences.

There can be no such thing, if we are serious, as a distinct separate youth culture. Every generation contributes cultural forms to the ongoing process of creating culture. There is no such thing as culture specifically belonging to a given sex. Language is the basic medium of culture and people, regardless of sex, share it. Ashanti speak Ashanti, French speak French, irrespective of age, or sex, or even class. Language is also a basic identity. It is language, spoken, written or signed that transmits culture. Class stratifications within national groups do not constitute a separate culture, but social class. Social strata within a given culture are but modified expressions of sameness. There is no such thing as an old people's culture or as alluded to earlier a youth culture, children have never been very good at listening to their elders, but they have never failed to imitate them, so much for the generation gap.

Culture is the unfolding drama of history. Language and emotional histories are examples of cultural dynamisms. Like languages, culture is life, the way a given people struggle to discover a way to live. It makes life significant to its members. It is the outline of group characteristics, the ethos or underlying spirit. It shapes values and makes behavior fairly predictable. Without culture, people are not people; they are mere animals living in the kingdom. Culture is that part of the environment that is created by human beings. Neither God nor Nature makes culture, people do.

An Addendum: Some Connotations - Definitions - Impressions of Culture

- Culture is what makes us human.

- Culture is not your color. It is your behavior. All human beings create culture, and are in turn, created by it.

- Culture is the way you live, not the way you look.

- Culture is what generates most of your behavior, not biology.

- Culture is those ways of living that are learned, shared, and transmitted from one generation to another.

- Culture influences and often determines how people feel.

- Culture is learned behavior. First allegiances are learned from culture.

- Culture is dynamic, ever changing. It does not stand still or remain the same. It is adaptive.

- Culture will respond to what is demanded of it. Technology plays a powerful role in changing culture, ancient or modern. Social life lags behind technological innovations.

- Family, religion, economics, politics, educations, entertainment, law, labor, sexual behavior, and even war, are all aspects of culture. While culture itself is the complex whole of everything that we do in certain ways.

- Culture is the complex whole of a life way. It is the total embodiment of a peoples' experience. It shapes one's outlook and attitude towards life.

- Ethics, morals, and social values are the basis of any culture.

- Culture, not color, is the true basis of group solidarity.

- Culture is always changing, intersecting traditions with newly evolving ways of living.

- Language is the medium of culture. Language is what keeps culture and transmits traditions, customs, values and habits from generation to generation. Without language, there cannot be culture.

- Culture is artificial, meaning that it is not created by nature, but by people. Whatever is not the creation of God or nature on this earth is culture.

- Culture is a product of human ingenuity. God and nature gives humans the capacity to create and transmit culture.

- Human institutions are products of culture. Social organization, community and structures are bound by culture.

- Culture is both form and function. It is how environment is shaped or structured, around human activity. Culture makes a distinction between form and function. All families have the same function, to secure the protection and survival of its members. But the form of families can be different, e.g. monogamous, polygamous, polyandrous, extended, or nuclear. Culture helps us to understand the difference between the structure of something, e.g. house, and what it is used for, or its function.

- Cultures are not superior or inferior to one another, but they are different.

- Culture operates like chemistry, like matter and the changes it undergoes. It changes forms, but cannot be literally destroyed. What culture adds up to is anything that people make or do. It is anything material that people make; a house or a hut, a hoe, rake, or knife, a table or chair or a jet plane is culture. It is anything immaterial that people do; or think, believe, feel; it is habits and customs, mores and natures, ideas and myths, arts, and the knowledge that a people might possess. Culture is what you eat, how you dress, talk, walk, sing and dance. Culture is that part of the environment that people create. Knowledge is culture.

The History, Drama and the Confusion of Nationality

Because of the power of language and uses to which language is put, the concept of history can mean whatever one chooses it to mean. What is certain is that human beings cannot live as human beings outside of history, or whatever passes for history. In a word, groups of people are products of what they experience through time and space. No group or groups can experience life without encountering certain realities in the environment that is, interacting with nature (animate or inanimate surroundings), and with other human beings, both their kindred and people who are different.

History is very human; it involves the story of a people with all of their strengths and weaknesses, their progress, stagnation, or regression, all of their labors in thought and actions, their hopes, dreams, disappointments and pleasures. The essence of history is a study of continuity and change, a study of contradictions between the marvelous and the terrible. In general, history in its explanation of life, which revolves around what we have come to know as nationalities or people who are bound and defined by a time-space specific reality and the forces that bring them into being. The history of our species includes all people regardless of their particular background. Life and history are experienced in a variety of ways. History is always unique to a given group of people. The history of ancient people differs from that of their modem progeny in time and context, but the process remains the same.

In the process of history, different traditions, customs, habits, beliefs, values and convictions, evokes group solidarity. Nationality, like culture, is the unfolding drama of history. There were not always a people called Irish on this earth. There was not always a nation-state like The United States of America on this earth. There were not always people on this earth referred to as "Negros". These phenomena are too often produced by the fortuitous turns of history. Most of the 193 nations states sitting in the United Nations are fairly recent developments. Few modern nation-states can date back more than 200 years.

One of the ironies in this discussion of nationhood is the fact that, of the entities of people called nations, only a few members of the United Nations predate the existence of American "Negroes" as a single group of people. The nationhood of Germany was invented thrice; first in 1871, out of a number disparate tribes (Prussians, Hessian's, Bavarian etc.) by Otto Von Bismarck and it lasted in some form until 1945. Germans were not always one people. Second the West (U.S. and allies) and the East (U.S.S.R.) divided Germany into two nations, West Germany and East Germany, which lasted from 1945 until 1989 and the fall of the Berlin Wall. Third was the reunification of the two German states after the fall of the Wall until the present day. This geopolitical entity is now one Germany once again.

African-American peoplehood was in existence before there was a German State of any kind. That great complex of tribes and ethnic groups that were forced out of Africa were fused into a new and unique people as a result of the crucible of the so called "Atlantic Slave Trade" and thus evolved, from at least as early as the late 1600's within the boundaries of what eventually became the United State of America. A shared sensibility in religion, language, music, customs, habits, mores and bottomless collective suffering over almost four centuries is what forged the peoplehood of Africans in the United States. Out of this calculated trauma emerged the unintended emergence of African-American nationhood. This nation evolved, on the North American continent, within the context of an evolving American democracy as an enslaved population. African Americans owe their nationality to history, not as a self-conscious political creation such as the white American nationality.

This people then, came into existence before George Washington was born, before the Constitution was written, before the American flag was invented, before baseball, the dollar bill, Uncle Sam and apple pie. It seems strange, but it is true, that there was a people, a culture, a nationality already evolved within the boundaries of the United States called American "Negros", before the modern nations of Germany and Italy were born (1871), before the later artificial nationalities of Yugoslavia and Czechoslovakia (1918), before British imperialism created Nigeria (1914), and before East Pakistan became Bangladesh (circa 1975) and indeed before most of what are known as Third World Nations today.

A critical distinction must be made between a Nation and a Nation-state. A nation is a product of history, of the unchartered historical process. A nation-state is a political product, brought into being by the power of the pen. Nations created by the fortuitous turns of history emerge half consciously, out of a gradual and uncertain evolution, dictated more by the unpredictable events than by conscious planning. A historical nation emerges as if grown by nature itself. A nation naturally comes into being and is not called into being by a document or written constitution. No flag signals its origins, as were the hundreds of nations among the indigenous peoples of North and South America, Central America and the Caribbean. No one victory in war produces its reality. It is not so sudden. Its leader is no president or prime minister. Such nations are spawned by the powerful agency of war or by a great myth from the spiritual world. It arrives by the communal process, that is to say, by something that is intangibly shared, felt, believed, intuitively known.

A true nation is a product of unplanned evolution, a process that is partly improvised, like jazz music. A nation as a process is something old and new. It is something that happens in spite of the world. No calculated scheme makes a true nation. This is the case for African-American nationality/peoplehood.

On the other hand a nation-state such as the United States of America was, consciously called into being. The Declaration of Independence, The Articles of Confederation, The Preamble and the writing of the Constitution, which established the formal organization of government, represent conscious self-actualizing acts to create a nation-state. Hence, the United States of America, unlike the African nation confined within it, is a product of politics, a product of a decision arrived at by critical choice, ideological debate among competing factions, influence peddling, and finally voting to establish the state, i.e. a three-tier system of government. Thus, the United States of America is among the youngest of nations, and yet, it posses the oldest written constitution in the world (236 years). England, more than 700 years older that the USA does not possess on single document as a written constitution. The constitution in England (The UK) begins with the Magna Carta, to which many documents have been modeled after.

A nation-state, as we know them, is a relatively modern political invention. The foregoing is a capsulized impression of history and the way nationalities occur. Human beings make history as they are made by it. Human events, such as the birth of a nation and the careers that they fashion are the essence of history. Our memories and imaginations come through our images of national history. Every single person on this earth is a creature of some shared or national history either unconsciously or consciously. To wit: History is quite simply, another word for Humanity.

Addressing "Race"

It is encouraging to know that some of us possess the will to put the question of "Race," the bane to American social progress, on the agenda of public discourse. This is something we remain frightfully reluctant to do. No major politician, academic or public intellectual, except a tiny core of Black and white intellectual independents, have dared to broach the question. For the most part, the most influential political leaders and standard intellectuals speak the language of aversion, denial and evasion. We continue to pretend, at our peril, that we don't see what we see. "Race" is our greatest cultural myth. Racism is our national sin. It represents a powerful and irrational belief that violates the spirit of democracy, the very ideals of human rights. Indeed the myth of "Race" and the reality of racism has been the major dynamic in the Republic since its inception. Our vocabulary is inherently "race ridden". "Race" its influence on our thinking, is like the air, it's everywhere. Even when we are not talking about "Race" we are talking about "Race" and when we decide to sit down and have a candid discussion about "Race" we talk about everything but "Race".

In order to effectively attack and get rid of the myth of "Race" and the reality of "Racism", we must make "Race" a critical part of our studies in school curricula. The very idea of "Race" its rise as a concept in the modem world, should be a part of teacher training, in preparation for informing students, at all levels. Children should be deliberately exposed to the idea of "Race" and have it placed under examination by bold teaching strategies. In this way "Race" will be inevitably revealed for what it is, 'A modem social construction, a fallacy that is the basis of erroneous assumptions'. It is entirely possible for children to gain a good level of understanding about this demon if they are earnestly and sensibly approached in a classroom setting. By the time they get to college, they will already be in a learning mode that contests conventional wisdom about "Race" and its by-product, racism. The school must be a leader in helping to deconstruct the fantasies about "Race". It would do well for us to remember that school learning has had much to do with promoting a racist ideology in our national life. The school, public, private, and parochial has historically been a major agency in promoting the doctrine of "White Supremacy". Only the semi-illiterate politician, fundamentalist preachers and the magic of Hollywood come close to having the impact that the American educational system has had on the minds and hearts of America's people.

Like all ideas, "Race" comes from the intellect of people. Meaning and value is then placed on ideas, not the other way around. Our perceptions of who we are as human beings need not subscribe to a popular misconception that we are pleased to call "Race". As an idea "Race" can go the way of other demons like evil witches, and curses by the devil, sound thinking that challenges conventional wisdom can defeat it. Clear thinking will teach us that "Race" in large part is comparable to beliefs in a superstition, an irrational collective belief, which is based on a false premise. As a myth "Race" reflects the beliefs and gives sanction to the actions of society.... and myths perform the double function of serving as models of and models for cultural attitude and behavior. The noted cultural anthropologist, Ashley Montagu correctly views "Race" as "man's most dangerous myth." It will take creative intelligence, diligent labor, and some suffering to extract the cancer of, racism from the American body politic. The growth of democracy will continue to be retarded by the weight of racism until a critical segment of the American populace decides to say no to racism and yes to humanity. This question of course, cannot be solved unless there also is a healthy dose of the scarcest commodity in America - moral courage. It is true now as it ever was according to James Baldwin, "Nothing can be solved that can't be faced."

What is "Race"?

"Race" is a modern idea. Its wide spread use came into being about 300 or so years ago.

"Race" is a confused idea. It is often interchangeable with nationality and culture as well as biology.

"Race" is a superstition. It is modem witchcraft, as in totemist, possession, exorcism, haunted houses, and the number 13.

"Race" is a cultural idea. The concept of race exists in some cultures, but not in others. Less modern people seem not to have developed elaborate myths around skin color, or other physical attributes, as labels for who people are.

"Race" is a myth. It functions as an explanation that simplifies complex reality. It is based on a fallacious premise that behavior is inborn and natural, not acquired, like skin color and that the two are intrinsically linked. According to this line, the genes that produce skin color and hair are also responsible for producing the values, beliefs, morals, language and intelligence in a person.

"Race" is unscientific because it is inconsistent.

What can we do about racism?

Read. Reading is one of the simplest ways to broaden your understanding.

Join interest circles with the people who are attempting to grow out of racism.

Challenge the ideology, not just individual exponents, of racism whenever possible.

Identify racist institutions and condemn them. Camus, Sartre and Fanon entertained the philosophical underpinning that oppressors cannot condemn themselves for past injustices, and since self-condemnation is impossible, therefore I/you must condemn.

Create new and free social space that will draw together like-minded people across racial and class lines. Build institutions that offer an alternative to racist ones. Build parallel institutions that will shadow racist ones, and intermediary institutions to eventually replace dysfunctional, or racist institutions.

Work towards creating a new vocabulary, that is, a new way of defining, perceiving, and knowing. Discover words, ideas, and concepts that correspond to reality.

Join any social action group that is geared toward fighting institutional and cultural racism, and building a new, truly free society.

Appendix

American Anthropological Association Statement on "Race"
(May 17, 1998)

The following statement was adopted by the Executive Board of the American Anthropological Association, acting on a draft prepared by a committee of representative American anthropologists. It does not reflect a consensus of all members of the AAA, as individuals vary in their approaches to the study of "race." We believe that it represents generally the contemporary thinking and scholarly positions of a majority of anthropologists.

In the United States both scholars and the general public have been conditioned to viewing human races as natural and separate divisions within the human species based on visible physical differences. With the vast expansion of scientific knowledge in this century, however, it has become clear that human populations are not unambiguous, clearly demarcated, biologically distinct groups. Evidence from the analysis of genetics (e.g., DNA) indicates that most physical variation, about 94%, lies within so-called racial groups. Conventional geographic "racial" groupings differ from one another only in about 6% of their genes. This means that there is greater variation within "racial" groups than between them. In neighboring populations there is much overlapping of genes and their phenotypic (physical) expressions. Throughout history whenever different groups have come into contact, they have interbred. The continued sharing of genetic materials has maintained all of humankind as a single species.

Physical variations in any given trait tend to occur gradually rather than abruptly over geographic areas. And because physical traits are inherited independently of one another, knowing the range of one trait does not predict the presence of others. For example, skin color varies largely from light in the temperate areas in the north to dark in the tropical areas in the south; its intensity is not related to nose shape or hair texture. Dark skin may be associated with frizzy or kinky hair or curly or wavy or straight hair, all of which are found among different indigenous peoples in tropical regions. These facts render any attempt to establish lines of division among biological populations both arbitrary and subjective.

Historical research has shown that the idea of "race" has always carried more meanings than mere physical differences; indeed, physical variations in the human species have no meaning except the social ones that humans put on them. Today scholars in many fields argue that "race" as it is understood in the United States of America was a social mechanism invented during the 18th century to refer to those populations brought together in colonial America: the English and other European settlers, the conquered Indian peoples, and those peoples of Africa brought in to provide slave labor.

From its inception, this modern concept of "race" was modeled after an ancient theorem of the Great Chain of Being, which posited natural categories on a hierarchy established by God or nature. Thus "race" was a mode of classification linked specifically to peoples in the colonial situation. It subsumed a growing ideology of inequality devised to rationalize European attitudes and treatment of the conquered and enslaved peoples. Proponents of slavery in particular during the 19th century used "race" to justify the retention of slavery. The ideology magnified the differences among Europeans, Africans, and Indians, established a rigid hierarchy of socially exclusive categories underscored and bolstered unequal rank and status differences, and provided the rationalization that the inequality was natural or God-given. The different physical traits of African-Americans and Indians became markers or symbols of their status differences.

As they were constructing US society, leaders among European-Americans fabricated the cultural/behavioral characteristics associated with each "race," linking superior traits with Europeans and negative and inferior ones to blacks and Indians. Numerous arbitrary and fictitious beliefs about the different peoples were institutionalized and deeply embedded in American thought.

Early in the 19th century the growing fields of science began to reflect the public consciousness about human differences. Differences among the "racial" categories were projected to their greatest extreme when the argument was posed that Africans, Indians, and Europeans were separate species, with Africans the least human and closer taxonomically to apes.

Ultimately "race" as an ideology about human differences was subsequently spread to other areas of the world. It became a strategy for dividing, ranking, and controlling colonized people used by colonial powers everywhere. But it was not limited to the colonial situation. In the latter part of the 19th century it was employed by Europeans to rank one another and to justify social, economic, and political inequalities among their peoples. During World War II, the Nazis under Adolf Hitler enjoined the expanded ideology of "race" and "racial" differences and took them to a logical end: the extermination of 11 million people of "inferior races" (e.g., Jews, Gypsies, Africans, homosexuals, and so forth) and other unspeakable brutalities of the Holocaust.

"Race" thus evolved as a worldview, a body of prejudgments that distorts our ideas about human differences and group behavior. Racial beliefs constitute myths about the diversity in the human species and about the abilities and behavior of people homogenized into "racial" categories. The myths fused behavior and physical features together in the public mind, impeding our comprehension of both biological variations and cultural behavior, implying that both are genetically determined. Racial myths bear no relationship to the reality of human capabilities or behavior. Scientists today find that reliance on such folk beliefs about human differences in research has led to countless errors.

At the end of the 20th century, we now understand that human cultural behavior is learned, conditioned into infants beginning at birth, and always subject to modification. No human is born with a built-in culture or language. Our temperaments, dispositions, and personalities, regardless of genetic propensities, are developed within sets of meanings and values that we call "culture." Studies of infant and early childhood learning and behavior attest to the reality of our cultures in forming who we are.

It is a basic tenet of anthropological knowledge that all normal human beings have the capacity to learn any cultural behavior. The American experience with immigrants from hundreds of different language and cultural backgrounds who have acquired some version of American culture traits and behavior is the clearest evidence of this fact. Moreover, people of all physical variations have learned different cultural behaviors and continue to do so as modern transportation moves millions of immigrants around the world.

How people have been accepted and treated within the context of a given society or culture has a direct impact on how they perform in that society. The "racial" worldview was invented to assign some groups to perpetual low status, while others were permitted access to privilege, power, and wealth. The tragedy in the United States has been that the policies and practices stemming from this worldview succeeded all too well in constructing unequal populations among Europeans, Native Americans, and peoples of African descent. Given what we know about the capacity of normal humans to achieve and function within any culture, we conclude that present-day inequalities between so-called "racial" groups are not consequences of their biological inheritance but products of historical and contemporary social, economic, educational, and political circumstances.

[Note: For further information on human biological variations, see the statement prepared and issued by the American Association of Physical Anthropologists, 1996 (AJPA 101:569-570).]

An Experience to Understand This Concept Better
RACE: Are we so Different?

As a result of public confusion about the meaning of "race," claims as to major biological differences among "races" continue to be advanced. Stemming from past AAA actions designed to address public misconceptions on race and intelligence, the need was apparent for a clear AAA statement on the biology and politics of race that would be educational and informational. Also to help address the public's general ignorance of this concept, AAA has developed an exhibit on "race."

Racism has long been a deplorable element of our society. The RACE project helps visitors to better understand the scientific myths of race alongside the realities of racism. The project's expansion allows us to bring these important conversations about race and racism to new audiences and venues.

Alan Goodman
Co-chair of the RACE Project Key Advisory Group

The exhibition *RACE: Are we so different?* brings together the everyday experience of living with race, its history as an idea, the role of science in that history, and the findings of contemporary science that are challenging its foundations.

Interactive exhibit components, historical artifacts, iconic objects, compelling photographs, multimedia presentations, and attractive graphic displays offer visitors to RACE an eye-opening look at its important subject matter. *RACE Are We So Different?* is a public education project of the AAA that includes a 5,000 square-foot traveling museum exhibit, an interactive Website, www.understandingRACE.org, and educational materials.

Developed in 2006 by the American Anthropological Association in collaboration with the Science Museum of Minnesota, RACE is the first nationally traveling exhibition to tell the stories of race from the biological, cultural, and historical points of view. Combining these perspectives offers an unprecedented look at race and racism in the United States.

Below is the Message Hierarchy of the RACE exhibit

Primary Messages:

A. Race is not an accurate description or explanation of human biological variation.

B. All humans share a common ancestry and cannot be divided into "races."

C. The idea of race is a product of human history.

D. Race has been and remains a powerful social force commonly used to rationalize the domination of one or more "races" by others.

Primary and Secondary Messages:

A. Race is not an accurate description or explanation of human biological variation.

1. Racial categories have varied over time and place.

2. Human variation exists, but most of that variation does not correspond to standard racial categories.

3. Human variation is continuous and not divisible into discrete groups.

4. Unrepresentative sampling of human variation can hide its continuity.

5. There is more variation within so called races than between them.

6. Geography and our evolutionary history not race explain human biological variation.

7. Traits are independent not clustered.

8. Race does not predict ability.

9. The development of humans is a result of an interaction between the genes they inherit and the environments in which their development occurs.

10. Genes move around, even if the people carrying them don't move very much.

11. The relationship of racial categories to genetics and biology is complex and often misunderstood.

B. All humans share a common ancestry and cannot be divided into "races."

C. The idea of race is a product of human history.

1. Race was not discovered in nature but created by people.

2. Race is a mixture of arbitrary classification and ranking disguised as natural description.

3. Race is a modern invention that emerged during the period of European exploration and colonization as a means to justify conquest, oppression, and inequality.

4. From the beginning race has combined classification with social ranking.

5. Race has made it appear as though inequality was the inevitable and natural result of biological difference.

6. Although race began as a folk ideology, it was taken up by science in a search for measurable racial differences.

7. The assumptions of racial science helped shape its conclusions.

8. Recent science has rejected race as a valid account of human biological variation.

9. Whiteness and its association with privilege and power was a human creation as much as any other racial category.

10. Who was white and who wasn't has varied over time and place.

11. The census reveals the provisional nature of race through the changing racial categories and their uses over time.

12. Resistance to racial injustice is as old as race itself.

D. Race has been and remains a powerful social force commonly used to rationalize the domination of one or more "races" by others.

1. Race is complex it's okay to be confused and to disagree about it.

2. We all experience the effects of race, but not in the same ways.

3. Racial categories continue to have social and political meaning and to affect the quality of people's lives.

4. Embedded within our economy, laws, and institutions, racism has had cumulative and lasting effects that go far beyond individual prejudice.

5. U.S. laws and institutions have systematically privileged whites over others.

Author's Recommended Readings

One basis of research is reading books. However, like everything else in this world, books have their limitations. Is it 10 books or 100 that one must read to reward good research? Now and always, the short answer and what matters is the quality and content of the message that one wishes to expose. The question of "race," its meaning and value is perhaps the most excruciating question plaguing our national heritage. This question has been with us since the founding of the Republic. The Founding Fathers assured us of this in writing the original U.S. Constitution, which has since been amended. The damage was left undone. The idea of "race" is a confused and confusing idea. It has been a major part of human thought and action through much of the modern world, particularly the western world. The belief that some human beings are inherently superior to others has spread far and wide. According to the logic of its believers, nature or God, or both, made some "races" superior in the endowments of the mind, body as well as spiritual life. However, in recent years, this view has been challenged by modern science and common sense. Since Hitler's Nazi Germany and the holocaust and the unspeakable crime committed in the name of the master Aryan "race" many progressive thought leaders have awoken to this very dangerous idea. Ironically enough it was the horrible blood bath of the Führer that caused racist American policy makers to redesign its racist practices after World War II.

Historically "race" and the belief in it had produced more violence, misery, sorrow, more unmerited suffering and degradation than any other idea yet conceived by the human mind. It is at the apogee of "Man's inhumanity to man." World War II, the greatest of all wars was largely driven by the idea of "race" from the standpoint of the Nazi murderers. There is really no accurate count of the lives that were lost because of this single thing which captured the mind and imagination of otherwise "civilized" people; Germany was once hailed as the centerpiece of "European civilization," and yet men and women of that "great" nation were seduced by this powerful myth. The scale of carnage exceeds that of all religious wars of the past, which were inspired by organized religions. The extreme and numerous atrocities committed in the name of "race" cannot be overstated. Adolph Hitler and his henchmen had many admirers outside of Germany, including the Nazi Brown shirts in the US. Today, the idea "race" still looms largely around the world. It defines an epoch in human history far outstripping the bloody crusades of centuries ago. Gradually, but uncertainly, a few lessons were learned. Finally there is now a growing body of information and knowledge lifting the veil of ignorance, which helps some of us to think a little clearer and muster a little clearer moral sensibility about "race". It is now known that there is no biological reality connected to what we call "race". There are no discrete "races". The eight billion inhabitants of the earth share 97% of the human gene pool. The most meaningful difference among the peoples of the earth is not determined by skin color or hair form, but by geography, language, history and culture which are invented and inherited through generations of specific human groups. "Race" is an invention, not a discovery. Every individual is a creature of culture. Culture includes the total embodiment of a people's experience. Once again, culture is not what we call "race". Culture is an acquired characteristic, not a biological one. The concept of "race" is a relatively modern phenomenon. What we have been taught about "race" over the past several centuries violates the laws of science, and that is observation and consistency. That is to say to the life of Adolph Hitler and all of his adherents, living or dead – there are no Super Humans!

Understanding Race, Racism and White Supremacy

This selection of books should guide the more curious. The works listed are from different time periods on "race" and "race" thinking. These works will lead to you to a greater understanding of how the very concept of "race" gradually and uncertainly evolved in the meaning that most of us unwittingly carry in our heads today.

Race: A Study in Superstition by Jacques Barzum
The civil rights movement in the United States has elicited a spate of racist pamphlets distributed in hundreds of thousands of copies. In opposition to this flood of bogus "science" is Jacques Barzun, the eminent historian of ideas. He is concerned chiefly with the history of the racist "superstition." His book consists of a Preface entitled "Racism Today," and an appendix giving a brief anthology of "Race Thinking." The history begins with the eighteenth century, is carried through the development of "The Nordic Myth," its uses in the nationalistic and colonial wars of the nineteenth century, to racism and its uses in the twentieth century, "Racism Between the Wars," and to "Race: The Modern Superstition." Barzun is neither a geneticist nor a biologist; in fact, he takes a rather dim view of genetics and biology. He is doubtlessly right in that "Equality is not scientific, but a political idea, and it is valid only when one assumes it, as do the Declaration of Independence and the French Declaration of Rights of Man. All men are declared equal in the sight of God and under the laws of a free society; after which anyone may claim his equal right by establishing his identity as a man.

Man's Most Dangerous Myth: The Fallacy of Race by Ashley Montagu
Man's Most Dangerous Myth was first published in 1942, when Nazism flourished, when African Americans sat at the back of the bus, and when race was considered the determinant of people's character and intelligence. It presented a revolutionary theory for its time; breaking the link between genetics and culture, it argued that race is largely a social construction and not constitutive of significant biological differences between people. In the ensuing 55 years, as Ashley Montagu's radical hypothesis became accepted knowledge, succeeding editions of his book traced the changes in our conceptions of race and race relations over the 20th century.

Montagu is internationally renowned for his work on race, as well as for such influential books as *The Natural Superiority of Women*, *Touching*, and *The Elephant Man*.

This edition contains Montagu's most complete explication of his theory and a thorough updating of previous editions. The Sixth Edition takes on the issues of the Bell Curve, IQ testing, ethnic cleansing and other current race relations topics, as well as contemporary restatements of topics previously addressed. A bibliography of almost 3,000 published items on race, compiled over a lifetime of work, is of enormous research value. Also available is an abridged student edition containing the essence of Montagu's argument, its policy implications, and his thoughts on contemporary race issues for use in classrooms. Ahead of its time in 1942, Montagu's arguments still contribute essential and salient perspectives as we face the issue of race in the 1990s. *Man's Most Dangerous Myth* is the seminal work of one of the 20th century's leading intellectuals, essential reading for all scholars and students of race relations.

Statement on Race by Ashley Montagu
Montagu in this work called for ethnic equality, arguing that race is a social invention with no biological basis.

Race: The History of an Idea in America by Thomas F. Gossett
This book analysis ranges from colonial race theory and its European antecedents, through eighteenth- and nineteenth- century race pseudoscience, to the racialist dimension of American thought and literature emerging against backgrounds such as Anglo-Saxonism, westward expansion, Social Darwinism, xenophobia, World War I, and modern racial theory.

The New Jim Crow by Michelle Alexander
This book directly challenges the notion that the election of Barack Obama signals a new era of colorblindness. With dazzling candor,

legal scholar Michelle Alexander argues that "we have not ended racial caste in America; we have merely redesigned it." By targeting black men through the War on Drugs and decimating communities of color, the U.S. criminal justice system functions as a contemporary system of racial control—relegating millions to a permanent second-class status—even as it formally adheres to the principle of colorblindness.

Strange Career of Jim Crow by C. Vann Woodward

The book offers a clear and illuminating analysis of the history of Jim Crow laws, presenting evidence that segregation in the South dated only to the 1890s. Woodward convincingly shows that, even under slavery, the two races had not been divided as they were under the Jim Crow laws of the 1890s. In fact, during Reconstruction, there was considerable economic and political mixing of the races. The segregating of the races was a relative newcomer to the region.

White Over Black: American Attitudes Toward the Negro, 1550-1812 by Winthrop D. Jordan

This book lays out in encyclopedic detail the evolution of white Englishmen's and Anglo-American' perceptions of blacks, perceptions of difference used to justify race-based slavery, and liberty and justice for whites only. This book is the definitive work on the history of race in America in the colonial era.

The History of White People by Nell Irvin Painter

A mind-expanding and myth-destroying exploration of notions of white race—not merely a skin color but also a signal of power, prestige, and beauty to be withheld and granted selectively. Painter guides us through more than two thousand years of Western civilization, tracing not only the invention of the idea of race but also the frequent worship of "whiteness" for economic, social, scientific, and political ends. She forcefully reminds us that the concept of one white race is a recent invention.

Slavery by Another Name: The Re-Enslavement of Black People in America from the Civil War to World War II by Douglas A. Blackmon

Blackmon brings to light one of the most shameful chapters in American history—when a cynical new form of slavery was resurrected from the ashes of the Civil War and re-imposed on hundreds of thousands of African-Americans until the dawn of World War II. Based on a vast record of original documents and personal narratives, *Slavery by Another Name*, unearths the lost stories of slaves and their descendants who journeyed into freedom after the Emancipation Proclamation and then back into the shadow of involuntary servitude.

White Supremacy: A Comparative Study of American and South African History by George M. Fredrickson

A comparative history of race relations in the U.S. and South Africa seeks to explain the different paths each nation followed.

The Concept of Race by Ashley Montagu

A growing number of biologists and physical anthropologists have come to feel that the variations in human physique are continuous and gradual and cannot be forced into any rigid racial taxonomy. The present work is the most challenging expression of this viewpoint. The caliber of its 10 contributors alone would justify its widest distribution among interested readers.

White Protestant Nation: The Rise of the American Conservative Movement by Allan J. Lichtman

White Protestant Nation offers a penetrating look at the origins, evolution, and triumph (at times) of modern conservatism. Lichtman is both a professor of political history at American University and a veteran journalist, and after ten years of prodigious research, he has produced what may be the definitive history of the modern conservative movement in America. He brings to life a gallery of dynamic right-wing personalities, from luminaries such as Strom Thurmond, Phyllis Schlafly, and Bill Kristol to indispensable inside operators like financiers Frank Gannett and J. Howard Pew. He explodes the conventional wisdom that modern conservative politics began with Goldwater and instead traces the roots of today's movement to the 1920s. And he lays bare the tactics that conservatives have used for generations to put their slant on policy and culture; to choke the growth of the liberal state; and to build the most powerful media, fundraising, and intellectual network in the history of representative government.

An Hour Before Daylight: Memories of a Rural Boyhood by Jimmy Carter

Carter re-creates his Depression-era boyhood on a Georgia farm before the civil rights movement forever changed it and the country. Carter writes about the powerful rhythms of countryside and community in a sharecropping economy, offering an unforgettable portrait of his father, a brilliant farmer and a strict segregationist who treated black workers with respect and fairness; his strong-willed and well-read mother; and the five other people who shaped his early life, three of whom were black.

Carter's clean and eloquent prose evokes a time when the cycles of life were predictable and simple and the rules were heartbreaking and complex. In his singular voice and with a novelist's gift for detail, Jimmy Carter creates a sensitive portrait of an era that shaped the nation and recounts a classic, American story of enduring importance.

Notes on the State of Virginia (1785) written by Thomas Jefferson

Jefferson completed the first edition in 1781, and updated and enlarged the book in 1782 and 1783. *Notes on the State of Virginia* originated in Jefferson's responding to questions about Virginia, posed to him in 1780 by François Barbé-Marbois, then Secretary of the French delegation in Philadelphia, the temporary capital of the united colonies. Often dubbed the most important American book published before 1800, *Notes on the State of Virginia* is both a compilation of data by Jefferson about the state's natural resources and economy, and his vigorous and often eloquent argument about the nature of the good society, which he believed was incarnated by Virginia. He expressed his beliefs in the separation of church and state, constitutional government, checks and balances, and individual liberty. He wrote extensively about slavery, the problems of miscegenation, and his belief that whites and blacks could not live together in a free society. (Focus on the Chapter of Laws).

Inhuman Bondage: The Rise and Fall of Slavery in the New World by David Brion Davis
In Inhuman Bondage, Davis sums up a lifetime of insight in this definitive account of New World slavery. The heart of the book looks at slavery in the American South, describing black slaveholding planters, the rise of the Cotton Kingdom, the daily life of ordinary slaves, the highly destructive slave trade, the sexual exploitation of slaves, the emergence of an African-American culture, and much more. But though centered on the United States, the book offers a global perspective spanning four continents. It is the only study of American slavery that reaches back to ancient foundations and also traces the long evolution of anti-black racism in European thought. Equally important, it combines the subjects of slavery and abolitionism as very few books do, and it connects the actual life of slaves with the crucial place of slavery in American politics, stressing that slavery was integral to America's success as a nation-not a marginal enterprise. A definitive history by a writer deeply immersed in the subject, *Inhuman Bondage* offers a compelling portrait of the dark side of the American dream.

The Ku Klux Klan in Minnesota by Elizabeth Dorsey Hatle
Minnesota might not seem like an obvious place to look for traces of Ku Klux Klan parade grounds, but this northern state was once home to fifty-one chapters of the KKK. Elizabeth Hatle tracks down

the history of the Klan in Minnesota, beginning with the racially charged atmosphere that produced the tragic 1920 Duluth lynchings. She measures the influence the organization wielded at the peak of its prominence within state politics and tenaciously follows the careers of the Klansmen who continued life in the public sphere after the Hooded Order lost its foothold in the Land of Ten Thousand Lakes.

About Mahmoud El-Kati

Mahmoud El-Kati is a lecturer, writer, and commentator on the African American experience. He specializes in African American history and advocates institution building within cultural communities. He is an advocate of building one's humanity through the understanding of their own and others' culture, history and community. He currently lives in the Rondo neighborhood, St. Paul's historic Black community.

El-Kati is Professor Emeritus of History at Macalester College in St. Paul, Minnesota. Macalester College has established the Mahmoud El-Kati Distinguished Lectureship in American Studies in recognition of his scholarly and community work. This endowment is used to bring distinguished scholars to Macalester for an extended engagement that includes public presentations, classroom appearances and conversations with students, faculty and the local community.

El-Kati is a frequent commentator through a variety of mass media outlets locally and nationally. He is a regular columnist for the Insight News and the Minnesota Spokesman Recorder. He is a consistent commentator for the local radio stations KFAI and KMOJ. El-Kati hosts a weekly public affairs radio show called "Reflections and Connections" on KMOJ radio in the north side of Minneapolis. He also moderates a monthly viewing and discussion on various Black classic films at the Fourth Fridays at the Movies held at Golden Thyme Cafe in St. Paul. El-Kati is the guiding elder for the grass-roots group called Solidarity, which organizes various community engagement gatherings called the Karamu Forums.

El-Kati has written such books as *Politically Considered: 50th Commemoration of the Supreme Court Decision of 1954*, *The Hiptionary: A Survey of African American Speech Patterns with*

Critical Commentary and A Digest of Key Words and Phrases and *Haiti: The Hidden Truth.*

www.MahmoudElKati.com • Info@Mahmoudelkati.com

About Papyrus Publishing Inc.

Papyrus Publishing Inc. is a grass-roots, non-traditional publisher that operates out of Brooklyn Park, MN. We are slowly becoming a resource for the community. We are not a traditional publisher where authors submit their work to be published, nor are we a self-publishing business offering editing, printing, and marketing. We network and utilize community authors, editors, graphic designers, desktop publishers, illustrators and photographers to produce our products. If your profession is one of these skilled roles, then you are encouraged to submit your information and samples of your work to Papyrus for possible collaboration and/or referrals. We also partner with organizations, institutions and businesses to develop materials, curriculum and products that connect to our common missions. Our email address is PapyrusPublishing@msn.com.

Papyrus Publishing exists to produce and distribute relevant knowledge and information that can enlighten and transform our communities locally, nationally and internationally.

The publisher's recommended readings and materials.

There are literally hundreds of books addressing "race" and racism. Below are books and DVD's that are some of the most widely used by professors in their college classes and used by anti-racist organizations in their various trainings.

The White Racial Frame: Centuries of Racial Framing and Counter-Framing by Joe R. Feagin

Joe R. Feagin extends the systemic racism framework by developing an innovative new concept, the white racial frame. Now four centuries-old, this white racial frame encompasses not only the stereotyping, bigotry, and racist ideology accented in other theories of "race," but also the visual images, array of emotions, sounds of language, interlinking interpretations, and inclinations to discriminate that are still central to the frame's everyday operation.

Deeply imbedded in American minds and institutions, this white racial frame has for centuries functioned as a broad worldview, one essential to the routine legitimation, scripting, and maintenance of systemic racism in the United States. Here Feagin examines how and why this white racial frame emerged in North America, how and why it has evolved socially over time, which racial groups are framed within it, how it has operated in the past and in the present for both white Americans and Americans of color, and how the latter have long responded with strategies of resistance that include enduring counter-frames.

The Mismeasure of Man by Stephen Jay Gould

The Mismeasure of Man is a 1981 book by Harvard evolutionary biologist, paleontologist, and historian of science Stephen Jay Gould. It is both a history and critique of the statistical methods and cultural motivations underlying biological determinism, the belief that "the social and economic differences between human groups—primarily races, classes, and sexes—arise from inherited, inborn distinctions and that society, in this sense, is an accurate reflection of biology." The principal theme of biological determinism—that "worth can be assigned to individuals and groups by measuring intelligence as a single quantity"—is analyzed in discussions of craniometry and psychological testing, the two methods used to measure and establish intelligence as a single quantity. According to Gould, the methods harbor "two deep fallacies." The first is the fallacy of "reification", which is "our tendency to convert abstract concepts into entities" such as the intelligence quotient (IQ) and the general intelligence factor (g factor), which have been the cornerstones of much research into human intelligence. The second fallacy is "ranking", which is the "propensity for ordering complex variation as a gradual ascending scale."

Race: Are We So Different by Alan H. Goodman (Author), Yolanda T. Moses (Author), Joseph L. Jones (Author), American Anthropological Association (Contributor)

Featuring engaging essays by noted anthropologists and illustrated with full color photos, *RACE: Are We So Different?* is an accessible and fascinating look at the idea of race, demonstrating how current scientific understanding is often inconsistent with popular notions of race. Taken from the popular national public education project and museum exhibition, it explores the contemporary experience of race and racism in the United States and the often-invisible ways race and racism have influenced laws, customs, and social institutions.

Race Matters by Cornel West

Cornel West is at the forefront of thinking about race. In *Race Matters* he addresses a range of issues, from the crisis in black leadership and the myths surrounding black sexuality to affirmative action, the new black conservatism, and the strained relations between Jews and African Americans. He never hesitates to confront the prejudices of all his readers or wavers in his insistence that they share a common destiny. Bold in its thought and written with a redemptive passion grounded in the tradition of the African-American church, *Race Matters* is a book that is at once challenging and deeply healing.

Dismantling Racism The Continuing Challenge to White America by Joseph Barndt

Racism has reemerged, dramatically and forcefully. All of us -- people of color and white people alike -- are damaged by its debilitating effects. In this book, the author addresses the "majority," the white race in the United States. Racism permeates the individual attitudes and behavior of white people, but even more seriously, it permeates public systems, institutions, and culture. This book does not intend to attack or to produce guilt, but its message is tough and demanding. It begins by analyzing racism as it is today and the ways it has changed or not changed over the past few decades. Most important, the book focuses on the task of dismantling racism, how we can work to bring it to an end and build a racially just, multiracial, and multicultural society. Churches are not strangers to the task of combating racism, but so much of what we have done is too little, too late. We have yet to make a serious impact in the racism that surrounds us and is within us. This book calls us to begin our next assault on the demonic evil of racism. The result that it seeks is freedom for all races, all people.

White by Law: The Legal Construction of Race by Ian Haney Lopez

Exploring the social, and specifically legal origins, of white racial identity, Ian F. Haney Lopez here examines cases in America's past that have been instrumental in forming contemporary conceptions of race, law, and whiteness. In 1790, Congress limited naturalization to white persons. This racial prerequisite for citizenship remained in force for over a century and a half, enduring until 1952. In a series of important cases, including two heard by the United States Supreme Court, judges around the country decided and defined who was white enough to become American.

White by Law traces the reasoning employed by the courts in their efforts to justify the whiteness of some and the non- whiteness of others. Did light skin make a Japanese person white? Were Syrians white because they hailed geographically from the birthplace of Christ? Haney Lopez reveals the criteria that were used, often arbitrarily, to determine whiteness, and thus citizenship: skin color, facial features, national origin, language, culture, ancestry, scientific opinion, and, most importantly, popular opinion.

Having defined the social and legal origins of whiteness, *White by Law* turns its attention to white identity today and concludes by calling upon whites to acknowledge and renounce their privileged racial identity.

Uprooting Racism: How White People Can Work for Racial Justice by Paul Kivel (Author), Howard Zinn (Foreword)

Uprooting Racism explores the manifestations of racism in politics, work, community, and family life. It moves beyond the definition and unlearning of racism to address the many areas of privilege for white people and suggests ways for individuals and groups to challenge the structures of racism. *Uprooting Racism's* welcoming style helps readers look at how we learn racism, what effects it has on our lives, its costs and benefits to white people, and what we can do about it.

Uprooting Racism explores how entrenched racism has been revealed in the new economy, the 2000 electoral debacle, rising anti-Arab prejudice, and health care policy. Special features include exercises, questions, and suggestions to engage, challenge assumptions, and motivate the reader towards social action. It includes an index and bibliography.

Between Barack and a Hard Place: Racism and White Denial in the Age of Obama by Tim Wise

Race is, and always has been, an explosive issue in the United States. In this book, Tim Wise explores how Barack Obama's emergence as a political force is taking the race debate to new levels. According to Wise, for many white people, Obama's rise signifies the end of racism as a pervasive social force; they point to Obama not only as a validation of the American ideology that anyone can make it if they work hard, but also as an example of how institutional barriers against people of color have all but vanished. But is this true? And does a reinforced white belief in color-blind meritocracy potentially make it harder to address ongoing institutional racism? After all, in housing, employment, the justice system, and education, the evidence is clear: white privilege and discrimination against people of color are still operative and actively thwarting opportunities, despite the success of individuals like Obama.

Is black success making it harder for whites to see the problem of racism, thereby further straining race relations, or will it challenge anti-black stereotypes to such an extent that racism will diminish and race relations improve? Will blacks in power continue to be seen as an "exception" in white eyes? Is Obama "acceptable" because he seems "different from most blacks," who are still viewed too often as the dangerous and inferior "other"?

Race: The Power of an Illusion (DVD)
by California Newsreel

The division of the world's peoples into distinct groups - "red," "black," "white" or "yellow" peoples - has became so deeply imbedded in our psyches, so widely accepted, many would promptly dismiss as crazy any suggestion of its falsity. Yet, that's exactly what this provocative, three-hour series by California Newsreel claims. Race - The Power of an Illusion questions the very idea of race as biology, suggesting that a belief in race is no more sound than believing that the sun revolves around the earth. Yet race still matters. Just because race doesn't exist in biology doesn't mean it isn't very real, helping shape life chances and opportunities.

By asking, What is this thing called 'race'?, a question so basic it is rarely asked, Race - The Power of an Illusion helps set the terms that any further discussion of race must first take into account. Ideal for human biology, anthropology, sociology, American history, American studies, and cultural studies

Eye of the Storm (DVD)

A wake up call for all ages, this best-selling program teaches about prejudices using a dramatic framework. It provides an examination of the realities of discrimination as experienced by actual students in the classroom of third grade teacher, Jane Elliott, whose demonstration shows how quickly children can succumb to discriminatory behavior.

This DVD chronicles her, now famous, exercise where she divides her class based upon the color of their eyes and bestows upon one-group privileges and on the other group impediments. Her work endures to this day and this ABC production, decades later, still has a great deal to teach us.

Jane Elliott, internationally known teacher, lecturer, diversity trainer, and recipient of the National Mental Health Association Award for Excellence in Education, exposes prejudice and bigotry for what it is, an irrational class system based upon purely arbitrary factors. And if you think this does not apply to you. . . you are in for a rude awakening. www.janeelliott.com